IMAGES
of America

DELTA AIR LINES
75 YEARS OF AIRLINE EXCELLENCE

Collett Everman Woolman (1889–1966), credited as Delta's founder, was in fact an assistant to Bert Coad in the early days of the development of crop dusting. Woolman was chairman, president, and CEO of Delta at the time of his death.

IMAGES
of America

DELTA AIR LINES
75 YEARS OF AIRLINE EXCELLENCE

Geoff Jones

ARCADIA
PUBLISHING

Published by Arcadia Publishing
Charleston, South Carolina

Library of Congress Catalog Card Number: 2003110669

For all general information contact Arcadia Publishing at:
Telephone 843-853-2070
Fax 843-853-0044
E-mail sales@arcadiapublishing.com
For customer service and orders:
Toll-Free 1-888-313-2665

Visit us on the Internet at www.arcadiapublishing.com

On the cover: Selman Field, Monroe, Louisiana was at one time the headquarters and home of Delta Air Lines. This image, taken in Monroe on March 3, 1943, depicts a group of Delta people in front of one of the airline's Douglas DC-3s. Appearing on the back is Clarence E. Faulk, airline president from June 11, 1934, to October 29, 1945. He later became chairman, a post he held until his death on August 31, 1951. On the front, the female is flight attendant Mary Winterberger and on the far right is Capt. Tex Buice.

Delta's famous triangular widget was incorporated into the airline's color scheme and is displayed on this mix of plane types at Atlanta Hartsfield International in 1991. The first aircraft to wear this scheme was the DC-8-51 N807E, delivered to Delta in the spring of 1962.

CONTENTS

This is the logo of the Delta Air Transport Heritage Museum, Inc., which is responsible for preserving Delta's rich history and providing many of the illustrations for this book.

ACKNOWLEDGMENTS

The pictorial material contained in this book has been derived from two main sources: the author's own aviation photo library collection and the collection administered by the Delta Air Transport Heritage Museum, Inc. in Atlanta, Georgia.

Many individuals, mostly employees of Delta, have assisted in various ways in the gathering and assembly of material for this book over a number of years. Delta's director of corporate communications, Steven E. Forsyth, is prime among these, as well as Todd Clay at International Corporate Communications. James Ray and his team at the Delta Air Museum in Atlanta devoted considerable time and assistance. Without the efforts of employees and volunteers, both past and present, along with the Delta Air Transport Heritage Museum, Inc., this book would not have been possible.

Several previously published books about Delta have also provided helpful background information in compilation of this book, notably *Low & Slow: An Insider's History of Agricultural Aviation* by Mabry I. Anderson (3rd edition 1997, *AgAir Update*, P.O. Box 1548, Perry, GA 31069); *Delta: The History of an Airline* by W. David Lewis and Wesley Phillips Newton (1979, University of Georgia Press); *Delta: An Airline and its Aircraft* by R.E.G. Davies (1990, Paladwr Press); and *Delta Air Lines* by Geoff Jones (1998, Plymouth Press).

Geoffrey P. Jones
Guernsey, Channel Islands, British Isles
2003

6

Displaying the Skyteam logo to the rear of the cockpit window, this Boeing 767-400 in Delta's latest and current livery, first introduced in spring 2000, taxies slowly to the gate at Tampa International Airport in Florida. Designed by branding consultancy Landor Associates, the word Delta and the logo are featured on an entirely white background. The universally recognized triangular widget logo is retained but in a softer format with rounded edges.

INTRODUCTION

It was 13 years ago in 1991 that I first visited Delta Air Lines at their headquarters and major hub, Atlanta Hartsfield International Airport in Georgia. Before that, on many visits from the U.K. to the U.S., Delta and its aircraft bearing the airline's characteristic triangular "Widget" logo had been an omnipresent backdrop at just about every commercial airport I visited throughout the United States. When Delta inaugurated scheduled services from Atlanta to London (Gatwick) in 1978, the "widget" was a daily reminder to European eyes of the might of what had been a mainly domestic U.S. mega-airline. When Western Airlines inaugurated schedules to London (Gatwick) in 1980 and 1981, another slice of the United States airline industry—soon to become part of Delta—was also spreading its wings.

But Delta wasn't always an airline giant, and in fact, after the start of scheduled services in 1929, when it was called Delta Air Service (DAS), only a year elapsed before passenger services ceased between 1930 and 1934. Delta's ancestry can be traced back to 1924 and the start of an aerial crop dusting outfit, and it was the crop dusting side of the business that continued through these lean years of the early 1930s. Delta's dusting division continued in operation until 1966. This date coincided with the death of C.E. Woolman, Delta's founding father, on September 11, 1966.

On a different lineage, Delta's ancestry can be traced back to April 1926 and the start of airmail services by Western Air Express at Vail Field, Los Angeles. Becoming Western Airlines in 1941, Delta took over Western in 1987. Other major acquisitions by Delta included Chicago & Southern Air Lines in 1953 and Northeast Airlines in 1972.

Monumental growth and change occurred at Delta throughout the second half of the 20th century. In 2000, Delta was a founding member of the important SkyTeam airline alliance, embracing Delta, Air France, Korean Air, and Aeromexico, with Alitalia joining later and most recently CSA Czech Airlines. By the start of the new millennium, Delta Air Lines was the world's largest airline in terms of passenger numbers carried (120 million in 2000) and operated from the world's largest hub airport, Atlanta Hartsfield International. Delta, in common with the majority of the air transport industry, has reeled post-September 11, affecting traffic and profitability.

From the small beginnings in Macon, Georgia, and then Monroe, Louisiana, and a small five-passenger plane, Delta has grown to become one of the world's leading airlines over 75 years. This book celebrates these 75 years and the employees, often the interface between the company and its customers, who have helped to make Delta such a *tour de force*.

One

POWDER BEFORE
PASSENGERS

To comprehend the start of Delta Air Service, Inc.'s first scheduled passenger service on June 17, 1929, one must go back to 1924 and before. The south lands of the United States, namely Louisiana, Mississippi, and Georgia, were already a rich and extensive agricultural area, dominated by crop plantations with the predominant crop being "king cotton." As any farmer will tell you, where there's a rich and productive crop being farmed there is the associated pest who will thrive from the farmer's toils; in the case of cotton, it was the tiny boll weevil insect.

Two personalities came together in the southern United States to fight against the boll weevil in the early part of the 20th century: entomologist Dr. Bert R. Coad and Collett Everman Woolman. It was their joint research and drive that led to dry powder insecticides—lead arsenate and later calcium arsenate—and the means of spreading this by the use of an airplane. This, in turn, led to the formation of Huff-Daland Dusters, Inc. and subsequently Delta Air Service, Inc.

C.E. Woolman was born in Bloomington, Indiana, on October 8, 1889. His father was of Scottish origin, the McFarlands, and his mother from Kentucky. He attended the University of Illinois and won a scholarship for a degree in agricultural engineering. His interest in aviation started in college where he helped the pilot of an airplane that had crash-landed on the college campus. In the summer of 1909, he traveled to Europe and attended the world's first aviation meet in Reims, France. Claude Grahame-White and Woolman traveled on the same ship returning to the United States, complete with a rotary aero engine that was to be used at the upcoming aviation meet being planned for Boston. Woolman helped him to repair the engine onboard ship.

In 1912, after he had graduated from the university, Woolman moved to Mississippi to farm and was soon supervising the farming of 7,000 acres in the Red River Valley. In 1916, he was appointed as a district agent in north Louisiana.

Dr. Bert Coad, who had been closely involved with the Delta Laboratory in Tallulah, Louisiana, in 1909 under several different directors, was pleased to welcome Woolman to the team. Coad also had an early fascination with airplanes and almost certainly around this time took his first flight ride. With toxic calcium arsenate being used to try to eradicate the boll weevil, the perennial problem was the even and rapid spreading of the chemical over vast acres of land. Coad went to Washington to argue the case for more aircraft experimentation and as a result, in 1922, federal funds were made available and the services of the Army Air Services obtained.

Equipment and personnel were moved to Tallulah for experiments with aerial applications of chemical powder. Two Curtiss JN-6 Jenny aircraft with Hispano-Suiza (Hisso) engines and one DH.4B with a Liberty 400 engine were used. Initially, the Jennies were used for dusting and the DH.4 for aerial observation; however, because the Jennies were underpowered, the DH.4 was commandeered, proved more adequate, and resulted in other DH.4s being made available. An airfield was constructed three miles from Tallulah on the Shirley Plantation, which was owned by Walter M. Scott; this was therefore called Scott Field.

Early August 1922 saw the start of hundreds of experimental aerial dusting flights from Scott Field, mainly for the cotton on the vast and unobstructed delta flatlands of the Shirley and Hermoine Plantations. During 1922 and 1923, there was continuous development of the aircraft dispensing equipment and technique. Coad and Woolman were convinced that although the principle was sound, a specially designed airplane was necessary for serious commercial dusting.

One of life's huge coincidences then occurred. The Huff-Daland Airplanes Company had been founded in 1921 as Huff, Daland & Company Ltd. to manufacture both civil and military aircraft. Thomas Henri Huff was its president and Elliott Daland his partner. George B. Post of Ogdensburg, New York, vice president of the Huff-Daland Airplanes Company, was flying south en route to a business meeting in Texas. He made a forced landing near Tallulah, was introduced to Coad and Woolman, and was immediately convinced that their dusting experiments had far-reaching importance. In this he saw aerial crop dusting as a new market for selling his airplanes.

In 1924, Huff-Daland Dusters, Inc. was formed, largely through pressure from Coad and Woolman, with George Post as president and Lt. Harold R. Harris, a retired Army Air Service pilot, as vice president and operations manager. In 1925, Woolman left the agricultural extension service at Delta Laboratory and took responsibility for Huff-Daland's entomological work as a vice president and field manager.

Already in production in New York was Huff-Daland's basic airplane, known as the Petrel 5 and powered by a 200-horsepower Wright E4 engine, considered underpowered for dusting work. Therefore, a 400-horsepower Liberty 12 engine was fitted, the wingspan increased to 50 feet, and a hopper added, enabling it to carry 1,000 pounds of calcium arsenate dust; its maximum gross take-off weight was 5,250 pounds. It was known as the Petrel 31. At about the same time, Huff-Daland Airplanes moved production from Ogdensburg to Bristol, Pennsylvania. These early duster aircraft had no trim tabs, all control cable runs were external, and the vertical stabilizer was either small or non-existent, all resulting in a tiresome and difficult aircraft to fly. When Wright J-4 and J-5 Whirlwind engines became available, most Huff-Dalands were converted. The aircraft were nicknamed "Puffers" very early in their career, an identity that was perpetuated in the first logo of the Delta Air Corporation when founded. A few of these early Huff-Daland's soldiered on and were still actively working in the Mississippi Delta as late as 1948.

Flying operations by Huff-Daland Dusters, Inc. started early in 1924 centered around Macon, Georgia. The 18 aircraft available were distributed throughout the region, at the company's new headquarters building, and on the airfield being built in Macon. It wasn't a tremendous first year for the fledgling company, due to lack of publicity, plantation owners steeped in old traditional ways, and most of the plantation fields being small and unsuitable for economic and safe application of chemicals.

In early 1925, the company moved from Macon to Monroe, Louisiana, largely at the instigation of Dr. Bert Coad, who was still with the Delta Laboratories, taking operations closer to the center of cotton growing and of boll weevil infestation in the Louisiana–Mississippi Delta region. Things started to improve, the number of available aircraft increased, and some 60,000 acres were under contract. Dusting services were sold to farmers on contract at the rate of $7 per acre for five applications, including the cost of the calcium arsenate. For the first time, they undertook aerial dusting of peach orchards in Georgia and experimented with the spraying of mosquitoes in swampy areas in Louisiana.

Business flourished between 1925 and 1927 on many large farms in the states of Mississippi, Arkansas, and Louisiana. By 1927, Huff-Daland Dusters had worked more acres of cotton than all other competing dusting firms combined. A year earlier, Huff-Daland Airplanes changed their name to the Keystone Aircraft Corporation.

However, the seasonal aspect of the business led the entrepreneurial Woolman to try to diversify in 1926. He saw business openings for crop dusting in Peru and took the bold decision to ship parts of five aircraft to commence operations there in two of the country's most fertile valleys. Within a year, the demand for dusting had expanded to seven of Peru's most heavily farmed areas. The Huff-Daland Dusters used in South America were distinguished by the circular "La Llama Voladora" logo on their fuselage sides, a man riding on a llama.

Huff-Daland contributed their operating certificate from the Peruvian government to the formation of Peruvian Airways (Peruvian Airways Corporation), incorporated on September 4, 1928. They secured an airmail contract flying between Peru and Ecuador as the first United States–owned airline to operate in the southern hemisphere, using a four-passenger Fairchild FC-2 and commencing air services on September 13, 1928. Twelve days after its formation, Juan Trippe's Aviation Corporation of the Americas bought a half-share in Peruvian Airways, which by January 1929 became Pan American-Grace Airways or PANAGRA, which was to be one of the dominant international airlines for over half a century.

Business for Huff-Daland flourished in both the United States and Peru at the start of 1928, but when Woolman returned to Monroe, he discovered that the parent company of Huff-Daland was trying to sell off the dusting division in an attempt to bail them out of their increasing financial difficulties. Woolman and a group of local businessmen arranged financing and bought out Huff-Daland's dusting interests. The contract was signed on November 12, 1928; they paid $20,000 in cash and an equal amount of notes, acquiring all of the former company's equipment three days later.

The company was now entirely financed by southern capital, so they decided to change the name to Delta Air Service (DAS), and this company filed for incorporation on November 18, 1928. On December 3, a charter was granted at the Ouachita Parish courthouse in Monroe, Louisiana, with the new board of directors being Woolman, Harold R. Harris, Travis Oliver, and D.Y. Smith. Pat Higgins became the chief pilot and Doug Culver was head of maintenance. In recognition of the role played by Monroe at the foundation of this famous airline, Delta continued to hold its annual general meeting in the Louisiana city until as recently as 1999.

The name "Delta," which was to become one of the most famous names in air transport, was first suggested by Catherine Fitzgerald, a secretary who had come from Huff-Daland's headquarters in New York in 1926. She later became one of the first female executives in United States airline industry as Delta treasurer.

DAS took over the majority of the assets, including the aircraft and personnel, of Huff-Daland. While this transition was taking place, a revolution broke out in Peru, both sides looking enviously at Delta's aircraft. Woolman quickly arranged the sale of these planes to a Peruvian company and shipped everything else of value back to Monroe.

By 1929, the huge cotton plantations were wholly reliant on aerial treatment, and DAS was going strong, despite increasing competition. The company's general headquarters was at Selman Field, which had a single east-west gravel landing strip, and while dusting was their dominant business, they had diversified into pilot training and carrying the occasional charter passenger. The DAS fleet comprised 13 Huff-Daland Dusters, an OX-5-powered Travel Air 4000, a Command Aire 3C3-T, and a Curtiss Pusher.

DAS and its predecessors unquestionably mothered the vast, complex, and sprawling agricultural flying business. It was responsible for many of the advancements in equipment, aircraft, methodologies, etc. Its dusting equipment was continuously refined and improved, and in this way Delta was able to outstrip their competition. Delta also established other fundamentals for a successful commercial aviation operation, notably an efficient maintenance and overhaul facility, as well as a meticulous recruitment and pilot training program. Culver's maintenance workshop became the envy of others in the United States aircraft industry in the late 1920s; establishment of his and Delta's motto of "No Job Too Hard" set the standard for the rest of Delta's dusting company and subsequently for Delta Air Lines.

Early in 1931, Dr. Bert R. Coad resigned from his job at the department of agriculture and went to work for Delta as head of entomology and field manager. Expansion of DAS's dusting operations to service southern Florida fruit and vegetable growers occurred in the early 1930s, flying mainly from Homestead near Miami. An operation started in the Brazos Valley in Texas, and in 1931 and 1932, DAS moved into Mexico, dusting tomato and other vegetable crops. The Tennessee Valley Authority (TVA) in Muscle Shoals, Alabama, contracted with DAS for extensive mosquito control work, so DAS diversified its aircraft fleet, converting Travel Air 4000s, a Waco 9, and Stearman C3Bs to dusters. Despite the fortunes of the associate air passenger unit of DAS, the dusting division of Delta operated until 1966, when the airline's management decided to dispose of the agricultural division. Perhaps not coincidentally, 1966 also coincided with the deaths of both Woolman and Coad.

The historic Petrel 31, more commonly known as the Huff-Daland Duster, was the aircraft with which Delta's predecessor company Huff-Daland Dusters, Inc. started operations in 1924 in Macon, Georgia, and then in Monroe, Louisiana. This particular aircraft is a preserved example, now located with the Delta Air Transport Heritage Museum, Inc. in Atlanta, and was restored in 1967 by a team of Delta employees. It is on long-term loan to the airline from the National Air and Space Museum Collection at the Smithsonian Institution in Washington, D.C.

Part of the Monroe, Louisiana crew that helped get the young Delta airline off the ground pose for this group picture taken in 1928 outside the hangar at Selman Field. Note the portion of the sign, "Huff-Daland Dusters," on the wall behind the men.

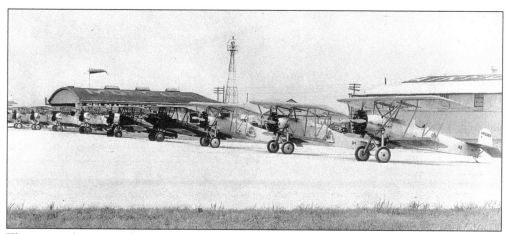

This image shows an impressive line-up of dusters at Selman Field, Monroe, Louisiana, c. 1929. Most are Huff-Daland Dusters, but the aircraft fourth from the right is a Travel Air 2000 duster, probably NC4316, which had a dark blue fuselage and silver wings. Huff-Daland Duster's fleet was at one time the largest privately owned aircraft fleet in the world.

A group of Huff-Daland Duster pilots chew the fat alongside a Stearman biplane in the 1940s or 1950s, believed to be in Monroe, Louisiana.

A trio of Stearman biplanes are shown during a dusting contract. The triangular logo appears here with the words "Agricultural Division" below it. The main cities of operation are also written alongside: Monroe, Louisiana; Bryan, Texas; Homestead, Florida; and Greenwood, Mississippi.

To help celebrate the 50th anniversary of passenger service and to honor the memory of C.E. Woolman, Delta's Louisiana ticket sales agent Jorge Sendra (right) sculpted a 22-inch bust of Woolman. Seen here in 1979 accepting the work is board chairman W.T. Beebe (left) and president and CEO D.C. Garrett.

Two

PASSENGER
SCHEDULES BEGIN

Diversification and growth were the key words in the 1920s aviation industry and were as significant as they are today. On June 17, 1929, Delta Air Service flew its first scheduled passenger service from Dallas's Love Field, via Shreveport and Monroe, Louisiana, to Jackson, Mississippi. Woolman had realized that crop dusting was fine but that the carriage of passengers and mail by air might be the means of transport for the future.

Already by the late 1920s, airlines such as Robertson Aircraft Corporation and Colonial Air Transport, two of the potpourri of airlines that would later unite as American Airways, then American Airlines, were flying. Similarly, Varney Air Lines and Pacific Air Transport, which were to consolidate as United Airlines, were doing the same. Western Air Express, founded on July 13, 1925, which was to become Transcontinental & Western Air (TWA), was already well established by 1929. The majority of the early flying by airlines though in the 1920s was for the Contract Air Mail routes (CAMs) following Congress's passing of the Contract Air Mail Act, also known as the "Kelly Act" after Congressman Clyde Kelly, in February 1925. This act established CAM routes for the carriage of airmail. No sustained passenger airline existed, however.

Charles Lindbergh's infamous non-stop flight from New York to Paris in April 1927 also contributed hugely to the realization that the era of practical air transport had arrived. The United States had unequivocally become "air-minded" overnight as a result of Lindbergh's achievement and then with his practical input as advisor to some of the embryo airlines and aircraft manufacturers.

Of equal importance was the advent of larger aircraft, the Fokker F-VII and Fokker F-10 from Europe, and then the ubiquitous Ford 5-AT Trimotor that enabled the mail carrying airlines to make a practical transition to the safe and reliable carriage of passengers.

DAS's Woolman saw the opportunity to expand his business, but needed something other than Huff-Daland Dusters if he was to transport passengers. In early 1929, the opportunity arose to purchase the assets of John S. Fox Flying Service, including its two, five-passenger, high-wing monoplanes—Travel Air S-6000Bs, NC8878 and NC9905. These aircraft were sold new at the time by Travel Air of Wichita, Kansas, for $13,500 each. The era of Delta as a passenger carrying airline had begun.

A relic of Delta's move into mainstream airline operations, their "Ship 41," one of the airline's original five Douglas DC-3s, first delivered in December 1940, has been lovingly restored by Delta employees. It flew again in Atlanta in October 1999 (see images on pages 22–25.) The DC-3s replaced the airline's DC-2s and remained in service for over 20 years.

In 1941, Delta moved its headquarters from Monroe to Atlanta, and the Civil Aeronautics Board (CAB) awarded Delta two new routes, north from Atlanta to Cincinnati and south to Savannah. Atlanta became the airline's crossroads.

Representing Delta Air Service's Travel Air S-6000B NC8878, which inaugurated passenger services on June 17, 1929, is this similar, Curtis-Wright Travel Air 6B Sedan from 1931, restored by Delta captain Doug Rounds and purchased from him by Delta in 1985. This aircraft is still airworthy and resides in the Delta Air Transport Heritage Museum in Atlanta.

Monroe's Selman Field is shown here as it was in the 1930s. Note the smoke marker on the hard runway to indicate to pilots the wind direction and Delta's general office building to the right of the hangar (this building can also be seen in the painting depicted next). This little stucco building served as Delta's headquarters until 1941 when the general office was moved to Atlanta, Georgia.

This painting by Robert L. Conely depicts Stinson Model A NC14598 in front of the Delta headquarters building in Monroe, Louisiana, in 1935. By this time, the name Delta Air Lines was in frequent use as a business title, although Delta Air Service appears on the building. The words "The Trans-Southern Route" are below the airline logo and on the nose of the aircraft is "U.S. Air Mail Route 24," (CAM 24). These aircraft were used for overnight services on Delta's trans-southern route.

Six Stinson SM-6000Bs (also designated Stinson Model Ts) were purchased from American Airways in 1934 and used by Delta to reintroduce mail services on July 4, 1934. The very first service on that Independence Day linked Dallas with Monroe via Tyler and Shreveport.

This image shows the first Lockheed 10-B Electra acquired by Delta on December 21, 1935. Six all-metal Lockheed 10s and one Lockheed 12 were the mainstay of the airline's pre-war fleet; by 1937, they had replaced all of the earlier Stinsons. The "20" on the tail was Delta's fleet number for this particular aircraft; in other words, the 20th aircraft that had joined their fleet, or ship No. 20.

Pictured in Atlanta c. 1939, where Delta's maintenance and operations department were already established is Lockheed 10 Electra NC14991. These ten-seat aircraft served with Delta until 1942 when all but one were requisitioned by the USAAF as UC-36s. Chicago & Southern also flew Lockheed 10s from 1940 until 1953, the year of their merger with Delta (see Chapter 4).

This Texas cowgirl is greeted aboard a Delta Lockheed 10 Electra that clearly shows the 1930s Delta logo with AM24 at its center (CAM.24). Agility was an essential prerequisite for passenger boarding in the 1930s.

Seeking a larger aircraft to supplement the Lockheed 10s, Delta acquired its first 14-passenger Douglas DC-2, purchased from American Airlines in February 1940. NC14275, ship No. 33, was one of four DC-2-120s that flew with Delta for just 12 months before being sold to the British Purchasing Commission in January and February 1941. Female flight attendants were first introduced by Delta with the DC-2; Miss Laura Wizark, from American Airlines, was Delta's first chief stewardess (instructor.) Birdie Perkins, a registered nurse, was the first Delta flight attendant in service on March 15, 1940.

Above, left: A Delta flight attendant models the airline's summer uniform used between 1940 and 1942. Clipboard and pencil were used to check off passengers as they entered the aircraft, in this case a Douglas DC-3.

Above, right: Delta continued to fly scheduled passenger services during World War II with a reduced fleet of only four DC-3s. This flight attendant models the airline's winter uniform, used between 1943 and 1946, while standing on impressively engineered boarding steps alongside a Douglas DC-3.

Delta's war effort centered around military aircraft modification and maintenance work. In May 1942, the company headquarters in Atlanta were designated a temporary Army Air Corps Modification Base. North American P-51 Mustangs were fitted with long-range fuel tanks, and Boeing B-29 Superfortresses built by Bell Aircraft in nearby Marietta, Georgia, received quick alterations. Delta's military aircraft modification group is pictured here with a Curtiss SB2C-1A Helldiver (carrier-based dive bomber) in Atlanta in November 1944 when Delta's staff completed the last modification work on 220 helldivers for the U.S. Navy.

Headquarters were relocated from Monroe, Louisiana, to this impressive new building in Atlanta in March 1941. The core of this building plus the hangar had changed little in 1947 when this photo was taken, and are still in existence in 2004 as the home of the Delta Air Heritage Museum.

Douglas DC-3s were being flown by every other major United States airline in 1940. Delta joined their ranks on Christmas Eve, 1940, when NC28341, ship No. 41, entered scheduled service. Ship No. 40 had joined the airline before this but was used only for pilot training. Soon, five DC-3s had been delivered, including NC28344 on December 28, 1940, and pictured here in Atlanta.

Passengers are shown here boarding a Delta DC-3 in 1941, while the porter loads cases into the rear baggage compartment.

The 1941 photo on page 21 was used by the aircraft restoration team in Atlanta to recreate a replica of the original 1940 Delta-style DC-3 boarding ramp, pictured here against Delta's ship No. 41, NC28341, now preserved in airworthy condition in Atlanta.

Delivered to Delta on December 23, 1940, their ship No. 41, NC28341, was sold to North Central Airlines in May 1958 at the end of its long career with Delta. It ended up in the Caribbean with Air Puerto Rico. A group of Delta retirees led the effort to locate it in 1990, ship it back to Atlanta in 1993, and restore it to airworthy condition. It is seen here during restoration at the Delta Air Transport Heritage Museum in Atlanta in 1998.

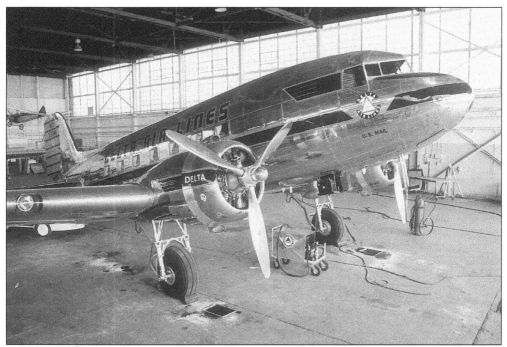

Delta Air Heritage Museum superbly restored DC-3 ship No. 41, a huge project coordinated by James Ray and a small team of full-time Delta employees, plus a huge army of volunteers. It is shown shortly before roll out for its first post-restoration flight in October 1999.

With Boeing 767 captain Bill Mercure at the controls, Delta's beautiful, DC-3, ship No. 41 restoration of NC28341 poses over the Georgia countryside. "[This is] probably the deepest and most thorough DC-3 restoration that has ever been undertaken," said project coordinator James Ray. Anyone lucky enough to see this DC-3 cannot fail to agree. It was also awarded the National Trust for Historic Preservation Honor Award, a first for an aircraft.

This image shows cockpit restoration of the Delta's DC-3 ship No. 41, although not 100 percent 1940s original because of 21st-century flight requirements. The central throttle and propeller pitch stalk levers and control wheels confirm the aircraft's vintage.

A huge amount of restoration time was lavished on ensuring the authenticity of the interior furnishings and finish of Delta DC-3 ship No. 41. Looking rearward down the sloping aisle, a 2004 visitor can quickly comprehend the ambiance that the 21 Delta passengers on board this aircraft in 1941 would have experienced.

NC28341 has been flown frequently since its October 1999 rebirth, mainly to promote Delta Air Lines at events and celebrations throughout the United States. It will be flown during Delta's 75th anniversary year (2004).

This nostalgic painting by Brad Driggers of Delta DC-3 ship No. 41 shows it flying over the airline's Atlanta headquarters in 1941 on the northern edge of what is now Atlanta Hartsfield International Airport.

Douglas DC-3s flew with Delta between 1940 and 1963. This post-war example, N25656, ship No. 56, was originally delivered to Pan American in 1940, went to Chicago & Southern in May 1946, and entered service with Delta's fleet on September 17, 1946, wearing the airline's new, post-war colors.

Eight Douglas DC-4s, former USAAF C-54s that had been converted to civil airlines by Douglas in Santa Monica, California, were delivered to Delta between February 1946 and April 1948. NC37472, ship No. 72, featured the inscription "U.S. Mail AM24-54 Air Express" in small lettering on the lower tail.

Delta boarded its millionth passenger in 1946. It was the job of an increasing number of female flight attendants—and the first male pursers—to ensure passengers' every need. This September 1946 photo shows that year's stewardess graduation class, wearing the 1943–1946 summer uniform on the boarding steps of a DC-4. By summer 1946, Delta employed 2,400 staff.

Three

1947 TO 1958

In 1941, Delta's route system linked only 16 cities: the trans-southern routes from Ft. Worth, Texas, to Charleston and Savannah via Dallas, Tyler, Shreveport, Monroe, Jackson, Birmingham, Atlanta, Augusta, and Columbia, as well as a northern spur from Atlanta to Cincinnati via Knoxville and Lexington. The Delta fleet was correspondingly small with mainly new Douglas DC-3s. In 1941, Delta carried 58,208 passengers.

Delta's assets grew during World War II; it continued to fly scheduled services, flew for Air Transport Command, and also worked on modifications to wartime icons such as the P-51 Mustang and B-29 Superfortress. An air cargo division was formed towards the end of the war.

August 22, 1945, saw the CAB award Delta authority to fly on the Miami-to-Chicago route. Delta had already purchased DC-4s and further DC-3s. It was the dawn of a new era. On October 29, 1945, the company's name was changed from Delta Air Corporation to Delta Air Lines, Inc. It was also the start of an era of continued competition with Eastern Air Lines; Eastern had pressurized Lockheed Constellations, while Delta had non-pressurized DC-4s, so Delta acquired DC-6s. Delta had an all-Douglas fleet, plus by 1948, interchange routes with TWA from Cincinnati to Detroit and with American from Ft. Worth westwards to California. Convair CV-340s had replaced older DC-4s by mid-1953, and Delta had also ordered the Golden Crown Douglas DC-7 to compete with other airlines' Constellations.

Non-pressurized Douglas DC-4s served with Delta between 1946 and 1953. One of their prime routes was Chicago to Miami, in direct competition with Eastern Air Lines. Eastern introduced pressurized Lockheed Constellations on this route, so Delta had to counter.

By 1959, Delta's aircraft were starting to appear in a new *White Crown* color scheme. Here, Douglas DC-4 N37477, delivered in April 1946, is seen in these new colors.

Douglas DC-6 N1904M has the ship number 604 on the tail. When Delta's first seven DC-6s were delivered in 1948 and 1949, they were ship Nos. 101 to 107. The pressurized DC-6 was Delta's competitive counter bid to Eastern Air Lines's Constellation.

Sporting Delta's *White Crown* color scheme, this Douglas DC-6 N1906M is ship No. 606, delivered new to Delta in December 1949. Delta flew a total of 11 different DC-6s between 1948 and 1968. This particular aircraft had the misfortune to suffer an undercarriage collapse on landing in Chattanooga, Tennessee, on February 15, 1968, and was subsequently written off. It was rebuilt and sold in Mexico as XA-TEN with Aerolineas Vega.

The continual need to stay ahead of the competition resulted in Delta seeking a DC-3 and DC-4 replacement, and they ordered 10 Convair 340s in June 1951. Much earlier, in 1946, Delta had provisionally placed options on the new Martin 2-0-2, but development problems caused these to lapse. Eventually, Delta had a fleet of 20 of the twin-engine, 44-seat Convair 340s when Chicago & Southern's were assimilated into the Delta fleet. N4806C, ship No. 306, was delivered to Delta in May 1953.

Maryanne Kowaleski models the Delta summer flight attendants uniform that was current between 1954 and 1965, pictured here in August 1956 with Delta's Convair 340—the *Cosmopolitan*—N4802C, ship No. 302.

Following the Convair 340 was the 52-seat Convair 440, *Metropolitan*. With improved soundproofing and other passenger amenities, Delta ordered eight in November 1955; the first, N4821C, was delivered in August 1956. This Convair 440—N4823C, ship No. 423—entered service on November 29, 1956, and flew with Delta until April 1970.

The Lockheed Constellation was considered by many to be the finest and most enigmatic prop liner. Delta surprised many pundits when it bought four of the older L-049 models from Pan American in 1956 to make up a shortfall in fleet capacity. The surprise emanated because Delta had recently disposed of the newer L-649 models that it had inherited as part of the Chicago & Southern merger.

This superb atmospheric picture shows Delta's Lockheed L-049 Constellation N88868, ship No. 502, taxiing to the ramp in Miami shortly after it entered service on July 5, 1956. These older model Constellations were expensive to maintain and marginally competitive when compared to the newer models other airlines were flying. Delta withdrew them from service in July 1958 and sold all four to American Flyers Airline in April 1960.

Passengers start to disembark Delta's Convair 440 *Metropolitan*, N4824C, ship No. 424, flight 428, via the aircraft's integral air-stair as the ground crew check the aircraft and baggage handlers swing into action. This early 1960s picture shows the airline advertising to boarding passengers that it is radar-equipped.

Malcolm Coldetz and flight attendant Zealiane Martin pause on the air-stairs of Convair 440 *Metropolitan*, N4828C, ship No. 428, which is operating flight 479—indicated on a small digital display near the top of the air-stair to reassure passengers they were boarding the correct flight—from Atlanta. The flight attendant is wearing Delta's winter uniform, current between 1957 and 1959. Some of Delta's competition can be seen behind, an Eastern Air Lines Martin 4-0-4.

Permission from the Civil Aeronautics Board (CAB) for Delta to fly between Atlanta and New York in January 1956 was considered the transition point of Delta from a regional service airline to a full trunk airline. It was also a major stimulant to the growth of Delta's Atlanta hub. Two of Delta's fleet at this time were the Douglas DC-7B N4883C, ship No. 713, and Convair 340 *Cosmopolitan*, N4807C, ship No. 307.

A Golden Crown DC-7—N4876C, ship No. 706—makes a striking pose. Ten of this model of DC-7 were operated by Delta between 1954 and 1968 and were used to introduce the "Royal Service," an improved and up-market level of in-flight catering, in September 1958. Delta had inaugurated service on the Chicago-to-Miami route in December 1945—DC-7s were used mainly on this route from April 1954 onwards.

Delta first publicly announced its order for the four-engine, 69-seat Douglas DC-7 in June 1953. N4873C was delivered to Delta in March 1954 and flew with the airline until July 1967. Introduction of the DC-7s stretched Delta's resources on all fronts from pilot and flight engineer training to maintenance capacity, proving extremely costly. Nevertheless, the spirit of Delta's management and staff ensured that "somehow it all got done."

A typically busy Atlanta Delta Day takes place in the late 1950s with, from left to right, DC-3 N1200M, ship No. 60, the last delivered to Delta in October 1947; two DC-7s; and DC-6 N1902M, ship No. 602. Delta's rapid expansion in Atlanta caused considerable pressure on the small terminal facilities there—a temporary "Quonset" terminal was operated from 1948 until 1961.

Delta established a freight-only unit in 1946. This followed wartime experience when DC-3 passenger aircraft with cargo bins were used for unscheduled cargo deliveries. From 1946, three former USAAF all-cargo C-47s flew predominantly between Atlanta and Chicago via Cincinnati until replaced by Curtiss C-46s in 1957. Five C-46Rs flew with Delta until 1967; N9874F and N9884F, ship numbers 102 and 104, are pictured here during loading operations in Atlanta.

Delta entered the jet age with the Douglas DC-8 in September 1959. The prop liners that had helped the airline develop into a major United States airline during the 1950s soldiered on until 1970. DC-7 N4875C, ship No. 705, is seen landing as Douglas DC-8-11 N806E, ship No. 806, wearing the new widget colors, holds on the taxiway in Atlanta prior to departure, c. 1962.

Four

CHICAGO & SOUTHERN
AIR LINES

New Yorker Carleton Putnam founded Pacific Seaboard Air Lines in June 1933, which operated Bellanca CH-300 Pacemakers on a coastal routing between Los Angeles and San Francisco. A year later, he applied to operate the mail service between Chicago and New Orleans via Peoria, Springfield, St. Louis, Memphis, and Jackson. After early difficulties, the airline was renamed Chicago & Southern Air Lines (C&S). (Putnam liked the substance of the name and its associations with the railroad.) C&S acquired Lockheed 10 Electras and started to fly passengers as well as mail on the route.

Routes radiating from Memphis were developed to Houston in March 1941, to Detroit postwar in June 1945, and to Kansas City in September 1948. C&S's first DC-3s were delivered in April 1940, and further ones in 1944 and 1945. The surprise award to C&S in May 1946 by the CAB of a route from New Orleans to Havana, Cuba, and on to Caracas, Venezuela, dictated orders for the Douglas DC-4. C&S added its first Lockheed 649 Constellation in October 1950. With Caribbean expansion from Havana to San Juan in January 1953, Putnam and Woolman were already talking merger, which was agreed by the CAB and signed on May 1, 1953.

For awhile, aircraft operated under the name Delta-C&S, but soon Delta's fleet rationalization saw Convairs replacing C&S DC-3s and DC-7s replacing Constellations. The merger, known as the "big breakthrough," propelled Delta from a small southern area airline into a regional and international airline. From Delta's single trans-southern route of 1929, Delta's network now spanned over 10,500 route miles into 20 different states and seven countries.

While the merger of Delta with C&S was generally successful, a Delta stewardess was known to recount an unfortunate incident when a lady passenger connecting from a Trans Canada Air Lines flight to a Delta-C&S flight in Chicago, who had apparently heard of the merger, saw a United Airlines airliner on the ramp and automatically thought "United" was the plane she should take!

Chicago & Southern Air Lines flew their first services north and south along the Mississippi River corridor from 1934 onwards. Like Delta, C&S flew Lockheed 10s, followed by DC-3s as traffic developed. The first of 20 DC-3s that they operated entered service in April 1940, and most transferred to Delta following the May 1953 merger. C&S's 1940s colors were a bare metal finish with orange cheat-line. NC19977, pictured here c. 1941, bears the inscription "Level Valley Aerial Route" on the lower fuselage beneath the word "southern." This aircraft was written off in Texas in March 1943 after transfer to the USAAF.

By 1952, C&S's colors had changed to green and yellow. Three of their Lockheed 649A Constellations are seen here in Memphis in the transitional Delta-C&S colors. The two Constellations beyond are in C&S colors but with painted white upper fuselage surfaces. All of the former C&S Constellations were sold by Delta in 1954 and 1955 to TWA and Pacific Northern.

Pictured in Memphis in 1955, Lockheed 649A Constellation N86521, ship No. 521, entered service with C&S in August 1950. In recognition of C&S's international route structure through the Caribbean and to South America, their aircraft were given suitably exotic names, 521 being *City of Cuidad Trujillo* after one of the cities on the route to San Juan, now more commonly known as Santo Domingo in the Dominican Republic.

Memphis was C&S's main hub on its routes between the Great Lakes cities of Chicago and Detroit and between the Gulf cities of New Orleans and Houston. Pictured here in Memphis in 1955 is a Delta DC-7 N4871C, ship No.701. Although C&S never operated DC-7s in their own right, following the 1953 merger with Delta, some of Delta's aircraft were delivered in 1954 in this joint Delta-C&S scheme.

Five

THE JET ERA

Appropriately, the 30th anniversary of Delta's first scheduled passenger service also heralded the arrival of the jet era at Delta. With its allegiance to Douglas, the order for DC-8 Series 11s was no surprise, part of a massive $110-million order that also included Convair CV-880 jets. On September 18, 1959, Delta became the first airline in the world to fly the 119-seat DC-8 on scheduled passenger services on its one-hour, 34-minute hop from New York Idlewild to Atlanta. Delta was able to steal a major advantage over east coast rival Eastern Air Lines, still operating slower turbo-prop-powered Lockheed Electras.

Delta was also ahead of the game again when their first Convair 880 entered service on May 15, 1960. Although TWA had ordered the type, financial problems precluded their delivery to this rival airline. Delta placed the CV-880 in non-stop service from New York to Atlanta, Houston, and New Orleans. The CAB's award of authority for Delta to fly on the southern transcontinental route from Los Angeles to Miami in March 1961 was the climax of one of the most bitterly contested route proceedings in the history of United States air transport.

Further orders for jet airliners followed, and Delta became the launch customer for the Douglas DC-9 in April 1963; remarkably, Delta ordered three examples of the anonymous Super Sonic Transport, or SST, in April 1964, even though the federal government had not yet selected a manufacturer for the type. Delta's first DC-9 Series 10 went into service with Delta in late 1965. Further DC-9s were ordered, and the larger Series 32 entered service with Delta in April 1967.

"Wide bodies" were the vogue airliner type during the 1970s. Delta had the distinction of operating all three of the available types—the Boeing 747, the Douglas DC-10, and the Lockheed L-1011 Tristar. It was Delta's surprise order for 24 Tristars, the "Ten-Eleven," in April 1968 that finally drew the airline away from its Douglas traditions; however, it was also this order that caused huge problems at Delta when Rolls Royce, the manufacturer of the Tristar's RB.211 engines, faced bankruptcy. Five McDonnell Douglas DC-10-10s were ordered in March 1971 as a contingency; they were then sold to United Airlines but leased back by Delta between 1972 and 1975. Delta's first Tristar 1s entered service in December 1973.

Fourteen Boeing 727-232s were ordered by Delta in March 1972, the first of a huge fleet that over the years totaled 196 different aircraft and, in 1981, made Delta the largest operator of 727s in the world, with 129 in service.

Delta beat rival airline United in being the first to put the Douglas DC-8-11 into commercial service, the historic day being September 18, 1959, when N801E, named *Pride of Delta*, flew from New York to Atlanta. The same aircraft inaugurated Delta's transcontinental jet service from Atlanta to LAX via Dallas on June 11, 1961. Pictured is sister ship N802E that also entered service on September 18, 1959.

The second of the new generation of jets to enter service with Delta was the Convair 880; Delta was also the first airline to put this type into commercial service, doing so on May 15, 1960, with N8802E. The Convair 880s were based at New York Idlewild and flew non-stop service to Atlanta, Houston, and New Orleans. N8806E entered service with Delta on July 7, 1960, and is pictured departing Atlanta in September 1960.

Perpetuating the golden crown logo of Delta's DC-7s, the Convair 880 fleet wore a crown above the "880" on the forward fuselage. The type stayed in service with Delta from 1960 until 1973 or 1974.

Convair 880 N8802E was named *Delta Queen* for the May 15, 1960 inauguration of the airline's service from Atlanta–New Orleans–Dallas–San Francisco. This aircraft was retired from service on November 16, 1973, and sold to Boeing along with the remaining 15 880s from Delta's fleet of 17.

Both the engines and colors changed for the Delta Douglas DC-8 fleet in the early 1960s. The original six DC-8s were the DC-8-11s whose engines were soon changed to more powerful Pratt & Whitney JT3D-3B fan jets and the aircraft designated DC-8-51s. Delta operated a further 15 DC-8-51s from 1962 onwards; N816E (shown here) was delivered in March 1965.

Loyalty to Douglas airliners by Delta continued and, between 1967 and 1989, 13 of the stretched fuselage, 195-seat DC-8-61s were flown. N823E, shown to be ship No. 862 on the top of the fin and front nose wheel door, was delivered in June 1967. Between 1982 and 1983, Delta's fleet of DC-8-61s were converted to DC-8-71s by fitting CFM56-2 engines. Under an interchange agreement with Pan American, Delta flew its first transatlantic flights from Atlanta to London using DC-8-33s on May 29, 1964. Passengers could fly from New Orleans via Atlanta to London four times a week and to Paris three times a week.

Pictured is the dream that never was, a Delta supersonic transport (SST). In April 1964, Delta joined the airline bandwagon and ordered three of America's SSTs even before the manufacturer and design was detailed. By February 1969, the Boeing 2707 SST became the country's preferred SST entry, the same year that the Anglo-French Concorde SST made its first flight. However, on March 24, 1971, the U.S. SST was cancelled by the Senate, who voted against any further funding for the project.

Seventeen Douglas DC-9-14s were delivered to Delta between October 1965 and 1970 as the Delta-Douglas synergy continued. Delta was also the first airline to take delivery of the DC-9-14 on October 7, 1965, when N3304L was named *Delta Prince*. The first scheduled service by a Delta DC-9-14 was on December 8, 1965. N3302L, delivered in June 1966, is seen here departing Atlanta.

The DC-9 fit the expanding Delta short and medium haul route structure well, and in 1965, an order followed for a further 63 of the 89-seat Douglas DC-9-32s. N3340L, pictured, was delivered to Delta in September 1968 and many stayed in service well past 1990.

Atlanta, Georgia's airport played a pivotal role in Delta's history, becoming the airline's headquarters in 1941. In June 1960, work on the airport's prestigious new terminal was well advanced. This was located on the north side of the current Atlanta Hartsfield International Airport, close to the current general aviation terminal.

While Delta Air Lines has dominated operations at the airport, they have never had it entirely their own way. Eastern Air Lines was almost as dominant here until their demise in 1991, and AirTran Airways is growing their operation in competition with Delta most recently. This 1964 picture shows two DC-8-51s—note the subtitle "Fanjet" added on the tail—in front of Atlanta's prestigious new terminal building.

Here is another picture of an extremely busy and crowded Delta ramp area in Atlanta in the early 1960s with a DC-6, Convair 440, and Convair 880 jet. It was Atlanta's mayor William B. Hartsfield who praised the airline's initiative in developing Atlanta to become the fifth largest airport (measured by air traffic) in the United States. Atlanta's airport later adopted Hartsfield's name for what became the world's busiest airport in 2000, largely thanks to Delta Air Lines.

This 1967 view of the Atlanta airport looks northeast towards Stone Mountain. Although Atlanta was Delta's corporate headquarters, it was also a stronghold of Eastern Air Lines until their bankruptcy. By the early 1970s, Atlanta was the third largest airport in the United States with around 7 million passenger enplanements per annum, 46 percent of them with Delta.

Delta flight attendant Donna King models the airline's new summer uniform in Atlanta in the spring of 1966; it was current between 1966 and 1968. A fleet Convair 880, *The Aristocrat of Jets*, is the backdrop. The year 1966 was also the year of C.E. Woolman's death, when the airline he had founded and nurtured was employing 13,000 staff system-wide.

On October 25, 1970, Delta inaugurated its first transcontinental Boeing 747-132 service from Atlanta to LAX via Dallas in competition with National Airlines, who also flew the southern transcontinental route.

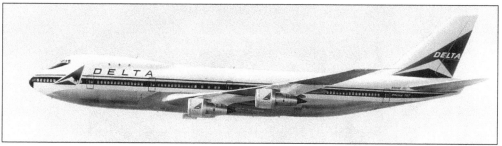

Pan American first introduced the Boeing 747 "Jumbo Jet" to airline service on January 22, 1970. TWA, American, United, National, Northwest, Eastern, Continental, and Braniff all ordered 747s for domestic United States operations, so Delta had to respond. It flew five examples between 1970 and 1977 and used them on the PanAm interchange services to London Heathrow instead of DC-8s.

Delta's first Douglas DC-10-10, N601DA, was leased from United beginning in October 1972. Delta's large widget logo, used between 1962 and 1997, can be seen clearly here.

Delta flew five examples of the DC-10-10 up until May 1975. It was delivery problems with Delta's Lockheed L-1011 Tristar order that precipitated the need to lease these five DC-10s from United. N605DA is pictured departing Douglas's DC-10 facility in Long Beach, California.

After the Curtiss C-46s were retired from Delta's cargo unit, the Lockheed L-100, the civilian version of the famous C-130 Hercules military transport, served as a replacement. The first L-100, N9268R, is pictured; it entered service on September 15, 1966, with the words "Delta Air Freighter" within the widget logo on the tail.

As the belly-hold freight capacity of the wide-body fleet of 747s and DC-10s came on line, the need for dedicated freighters diminished. Delta's fleet of eight L-100s (including two leased from Lockheed in 1968 and 1969) was finally retired in September 1973. This example features under-wing auxiliary fuel tanks for increased range.

Introduced in 1962, Delta's widget in oval logo shows the outer oval in red and the large "Delta Air Lines" on a dark blue background.

During the American bicentennial celebrations in 1976, Delta introduced a special celebratory widget logo for some of its fleet.

From the "swinging 60s" to the "splendid 70s," these Delta flight attendants model a range of casual styles worn between 1970 and 1973, including the first accepted use of trousers or slacks. The backdrop is a Douglas DC-8, N803E. By 1977, Delta employed 28,527 staff system-wide and was flying 18,042,339,000 revenue passenger miles per annum.

Six

NORTHEAST
AIRLINES

Delta's bid to consolidate its position in the Northeast and on New York–to–Florida routes was the beginning of its takeover of Northeast Airlines in 1971. Northwest Airlines had already tried, along with Eastern and TWA. President Nixon finally approved the merger on May 19, 1972, and it came into effect on August 1. Northeast's Yellowbird fleet numbered some 45 aircraft, with Convair 880s, Boeing 727-95s and -295s, and DC-9-31s.

Northeast's history can be traced back to the late 1920s and the Boston-Maine Railroad and Maine Central Railroad. Boston-Maine Airways began experimental operation under contract by Pan American Airways in July 1931. A group of businessmen and the famous pilot Amelia Earhart founded National Airways and contracted with Boston-Maine to begin service on August 11, 1933, and again later that year with Central Vermont Airways. In November 1940, Boston-Maine Airways and Central Vermont Airways became Northeast Airlines.

Mayflower Airlines was founded in Boston in 1936, and the Airline Feeder System in New Jersey and Connecticut in October 1937. Northeast Airlines took over the route authorities from these failed operators in June 1944, having already established Lockheed 10A Electra and DC-2 services throughout much of New England. Northeast Airlines had also contributed hugely to the war effort, operating DC-3s (C-53s) in the Canadian Arctic and even across the Atlantic during World War II.

During the late 1940s and the 1950s, Northeast expanded, adding first DC-4s, then DC-6Bs, along with Convair 240s. Attractions to British-built airliners saw Northeast close to buying a fleet of Bristol Britannia long-range turbo-props in the mid-1950s. Cancelled in June 1958, the British connection materialized later that year with the first of Northeast's order for 10 Vickers V.798D Viscount, four-engine turbo-props. Northeast was thus able to hold its own on the competitive Boston-New York corridor. Northeast leased a Boeing 707-331 from TWA and beat Eastern when it inaugurated jet service to Florida in December 1959.

Northeast was an early pioneer in the United States of the commuter or feeder service. From small northeastern communities, it used its seven Fairchild-Hiller FH.227B (the United States version of the Dutch-built F.27 Friendship) from July 1966 onwards, on routes that were not economical for jets (see Chapter Nine). These FH-227s passed to Delta.

The name of Northeast Airlines was formally adopted on November 19, 1940, and the airline's first Douglas DC-3 delivered in May 1941 for a network of routes radiating from Boston to Montreal, Caribou (Maine), and Moncton (New Brunswick), via Bangor (Maine). N45388, pictured here in the 1950s, was one of a fleet of 24 that Northeast flew—including military C-53s—between 1941 and 1967.

This DC-3 was delivered to Northeast on May 8, 1941, but was traded to TWA the following year—along with two others—for smaller DC-2s. During the 1990s, a group of enthusiasts obtained this historic aircraft and refurbished it to airworthy condition, flying it to U.S. air shows. It is seen here in April 1998 at the Sun 'n Fun Fly-In in Lakeland, Florida.

Northeast flew ten Convair 240s, with the first—N91237—delivered on February 25, 1949. They operated for up ten years on Northeast's short sector, an intense network of routes throughout New England, centered on their Boston headquarters.

54

Seventeen Douglas DC-6Bs were operated by Northeast between 1957 and 1967. Designated *Sunliner* on the tail, this 80-seat type was used by the airline to inaugurate services from Boston via New York to Miami from January 1957, although a DC-6A had actually been used for the very first service. This is N6589C, delivered on October 15, 1957.

Northeast's Pilgrim logo is clearly displayed beneath the captain's window of the airline's first Douglas DC-6B, N6580C. Prior to the delivery of Northeast's own DC-6s, the airline leased one DC-6A from Flying Tiger Line.

For two years after August 1958, when the first British-built, turbo-prop Vickers V.798D Viscounts were delivered to Northeast, they were able to increase their market share in the Boston–New York–Washington corridor market from 8 percent to 35 percent. In April 1961, Eastern Air Lines introduced their Air Shuttle with Lockheed Electras, to Northeast's detriment. Viscount N6595C is seen here with the competition's Electra.

Howard Hughes took control of Northeast in mid-1962 until 1964, one of many mergers, takeovers, and other negotiations that Northeast was subject to at the time. Between 1960 and 1966, Hughes Tool leased six Convair 880s, part of a fleet of ten the airline used until 1972. In 1967 and 1968, a single Convair 990 was also leased.

The Storer Broadcasting Company from Miami took over the majority shareholding of Northeast from Howard Hughes in 1965 and immediately ordered 33 new jets, including new Boeing 727 tri-jets. N1633 was one of the eight, short-body 727-95s wearing the striking—and for its time revolutionary—Loewy-designed yellow styling that soon attracted the nomenclature of "yellowbird."

In characteristic *Northeast Yellowbird* colors, Northeast Boeing 727-95 N1637 was one of eight such models used between 1965 and 1972, the year of the merger with Delta.

Following the 1972 approval of the merger of Northeast with Delta, a substantial number of Northeast's aircraft were assimilated into the Delta fleet, including Boeing 727s, Douglas DC-9s, and Fairchild-Hiller FH.227s. Seen here in Atlanta in Delta's colors is Northeast's very first Boeing 727-95 N1631, which entered service with Delta prior to the arrival of its own order for 727-232 Advanced. This particular aircraft was eventually sold by Delta in September 1977.

Northeast's Douglas DC-9-31 N978NE, shown here taxiing at Washington National (now Washington Ronald Reagan), entered service in November 1967 and was eventually sold by Delta to Ozark Airlines in 1975. Northeast's 12 DC-9-31s replaced its Douglas DC-6Bs.

Passengers are shown here boarding a Northeast Douglas DC-9-31. Northeast's history in the 1950s and 1960s was a roller-coaster ride of several crashes, potential mergers, financial troubles, and takeovers. In November 1969, Northwest Airlines planned to merge with Northeast, approved on December 31, 1970, but Northwest withdrew on March 10, 1971. Delta immediately submitted their merger proposals.

A Commuter Yellowbird Fairchild-Hiller FH. 227, one of seven of this United States derivative of the Dutch-built Fokker F.27 Friendship, was ideally suited to Northeast's dense, short-sector network in New England. This photo must have been taken in 1972, shortly after the Northeast-Delta merger, as it carries a Delta widget logo on the forward fuselage.

The same ex-Northeast FH.227 aircraft as in the previous photo—N378NE—is shown here in a full Delta color scheme. The first Northeast FH.227 was delivered in July 1966 and, following the Delta merger, six of them continued to operate with Delta until 1975.

Seven

TRANSATLANTIC
AND BEYOND

In December 1963, the CAB agreed an interchange agreement between Delta and Pan American Airways, which permitted Delta to fly through service from New Orleans and Atlanta to London Heathrow via Washington, D.C., under the auspices of PanAm, using DC-8s. When Delta's Boeing 747-132s were delivered in 1970 and 1971, they were frequently used on PanAm interchange services to London Heathrow.

It was the Lockheed Tristar, though, that was intended to forge the Atlanta airline's international expansion. The CAB awarded Delta its first transatlantic route in December 1977 as part of a new round of bilateral route negotiations between the U.K. and the U.S. British Caledonian was awarded rights between Houston and London Gatwick, and Delta between Atlanta and London Gatwick. Two TWA Tristar 200s were leased to get the service operational, and the inaugural service was flown from Atlanta on April 30, 1978. Delta's own longer range Tristar 500s took over the service in June 1979, at the same time as an Atlanta-to-Frankfurt service was inaugurated. Delta eventually had a fleet of 54 Tristars, the last of which was retired from commercial service on July 31, 2001. (It was donated to The Flying Hospital, a non-profit airborne medical and surgical facility.)

The year 1978 was also a watershed in the United States air transport industry when Congress passed the Airline Deregulation Act, signed by President Carter on October 24. Thirty new airlines joined the regional airline ranks in the United States in the first post-deregulation year. Competition was intense and non-profitability followed. Nevertheless, Boeing perceived requirements for new types and Delta was quick to appreciate the importance of a modern and efficient fleet. Along with American, Delta became launch customer for the new Boeing 767-200, introducing it on transcontinental flights in December 1982. Perceived as a 727 successor (and DC-9 to a lesser extent), Delta also ordered Boeing 757-232s, with their first example entering service in November 1984.

Delta's tradition and keenness to stick with Douglas's successor McDonnell Douglas meant assurance of their interest in the new Super 80 version of the DC-9, the MD-88. Before such, however, in the early 1980s, Delta ordered its first Boeing 737-200s for service entry in November 1983. (The first MD-88s of an initial fleet total of 67 aircraft did not join Delta until December 1987.) These 1980s jet deliveries all perpetuated Delta's triangular widget logo and a color scheme that had not changed significantly since the early 1960s.

The first Lockheed L-1011 Tristar 1 to enter service with Delta was in December 1973, five years after Delta's surprise order for the Lockheed wide-body tri-jet. Here Tristar 1 N728DA, a type that rarely visited London, is seen at Gatwick. Delta operated the most Tristars of any airline in the world, and at one time in the 1990s, had 56 in its fleet.

This Tristar—or "ten-eleven"—is seen amidst the sub-tropics of the Ft. Lauderdale-Hollywood International Airport in Florida. The 250-seat wide-body was used extensively by Delta to serve the popular Florida vacation destinations, including Orlando, Ft. Lauderdale, Tampa, and Miami.

The CAB's award to Delta of route authority between Atlanta and London (Gatwick) occurred on December 21, 1977. The inaugural service from Atlanta necessitated a longer-range version than the Tristar 1s, so pending the delayed delivery of its own Tristar 500s, Delta leased two Tristar 200s from TWA between April 1978 and 1980. These were N81028 and N81029, the former seen departing Atlanta for the London inaugural flight.

The first L-1011 Tristar 500 was delivered to Delta in May 1979 in time to inaugurate the second Delta transatlantic schedule from Atlanta to Frankfurt, Germany, in June 1979. One of the Tristar 500s, N752DA, is seen here at London (Gatwick) in 1983. On July 31, 2001, the last scheduled Delta flight, DL1949, was operated between Orlando and Atlanta with Tristar 1 N728DA, an aircraft that first flew on November 9, 1979, and entered service with Delta on February 18, 1980.

When Congress passed the Airline Deregulation Act in 1978, fare wars between the major U.S. airlines became intense. Having the correct aircraft for the job was important. In 1983, Delta traded 11 of its Tristar 1 fleet to Boeing as part of a deal to purchase 33 Boeing 737-232s. They were used primarily to grow Delta's new Dallas–Ft. Worth hub in competition with American. Further 737s joined the Delta fleet following the merger with Western Airlines in 1987.

In 1972, Delta placed an order for another of Boeing's new jets, the three-engine Boeing 727-232 Advanced. The first example of 116 of its own arrived in January 1973, and by the end of 1981, Delta had become the world's largest operator of the 727-200, with 129 in service. N525DA, one of these 727-232s, is seen at push-back in Atlanta in 1991.

More 727-200 Series were added to the Delta fleet in 1987, following the merger with Western Airlines. This former Western 727-247, N830WA, is seen touching down in Atlanta in 1999, the historic "Fly Delta Jets" hoarding on the airline's maintenance facility beyond. Delta retired its last 727—another ex-Western aircraft, N283WA—on April 6, 2003, when it flew its last revenue service from Greensboro, North Carolina, to Atlanta, flight DL607.

The dominance of the Boeing 727-232 in Delta service is evident in this stunning publicity shot in Atlanta in October 1980. The majority of those aircraft pictured are 727s, but a few DC-8s and Tristars are also evident. By 1982, Atlanta was ranked the world's busiest hub with over 35 million passengers handled.

David C. Garrett joined Delta in 1946 and rose through the ranks to become airline president in 1971, then serving as CEO from 1978 to 1987, as well as chairman from 1984. His years as chairman were extremely difficult, the airline reeling, along with most other U.S. airlines, from post-deregulation losses as competitor airlines slashed fares.

Delta's first Boeing 767-232 was part of Boeing's prestigious display at the September 1982 Farnborough International Air Show in Great Britain. Wearing a huge "767" on the tail, to distinguish from the Boeing 757, which was also being debuted at the same show, this aircraft became the historic *Spirit of Delta*.

Delta, along with American, was launch customer for the General Electric CF6-80–powered version of the new twin-engine Boeing 767-200. Delta was already committed to a huge order for the new type when the early 1980s financial results were announced. Most U.S. airlines responded by laying off staff, but Delta did not. In recognition for this loyalty, staff raised $30 million from wage and salary deductions to fund the airline's first 767-200. It was named *Spirit of Delta.*

Spirit of Delta, N102DA, a Boeing 767-232, is still flying with Delta in 2003 and still wears its historic name on the nose. However, since the 2000 creation of the Skyteam alliance, it bears the Skyteam logo as well. *Spirit of Delta* flew Delta's inaugural 767 service between Atlanta and Tampa on December 15, 1982.

This plane, the smallest version of the Boeing 767 (compare with those pictured in Chapter 10), "cleans up" on its departure climb out from Miami in April 1998. Fifteen of this 767-200 series joined the Delta fleet where they are usually configured for 204 passengers—18 in "Business Elite" and 186 "Y" or coach-class.

Considerable similar to the Boeing 727, Boeing's new 757 also first joined Delta's fleet in the 1980s. Making its maiden flight on February 19, 1982, is the 193-seat, twin-jet Boeing 757-232. Delta was already the launch customer for the Pratt & Whitney PW2037-engined version, having placed an order for 60 in November 1980. The first entered service with Delta on November 28, 1984.

Delta's loyalty to the products from Douglas has been well illustrated in previous chapters. DC-9s played a prominent roll in Delta's growth and success in the 1960s and 1970s, ever since being launch customer and putting the DC-9-14 into service in December 1965. When Douglas became McDonnell Douglas in 1980, the Douglas DC-9 Super 80 became the MD-80. Here, N959DL, an MD-88, lands at Washington National with the Capitol in the distance.

Delta was launch customer for the MD-88, placing its initial order for 30 of the 142-seat twin-jets in January 1986. As many as 120 MD-88s flew with Delta, the first entering service in January 1988. Here, N958DL taxies to the terminal at a cold and snowy Cincinnati-North Kentucky International Airport in winter 2000.

Waiting for departure at Ft. Lauderdale-Hollywood International Airport in Florida is N941DL, an MD-88 powered by two tail-mounted Pratt & Whitney JT8D-219 engines.

"Widget-world," Delta's headquarters and primary hub at Atlanta Hartsfield International Airport at the end of the 1980s, shows a complete cross-section of the airline's domestic fleet at the time. From left to right are a Boeing 737-232s, a Boeing 727-232, an MD-88, a Boeing 757-232, and a Boeing 767-232. In 1987, Atlanta was handling a total of 47.7 million passengers annually, 90 percent with Delta and rival Eastern Air Lines.

As Delta celebrated its 50th anniversary of passenger services in 1979, new uniforms were introduced for flight attendants that were worn well into the 1980s. The significance of the 50th anniversary prompted Delta to shoot this publicity photo in Atlanta in front of the preserved Huff-Daland Duster.

Philadelphia-based Ransome Airlines became part of Delta's commuter airline system, Delta Connection (see Chapter 9), in March 1984. It operated services in the northeastern United States on behalf of Delta with a fleet of eight DeHavilland Canada DHC-7-102s (Dash 7s) and four Mohawk 298s. DHC-7 N176RA is seen here in New York in front of a Delta Tristar and Boeing 727. Ransome was sold to PanAm in the late 1980s.

The Londoner, N821L, a Douglas DC-10-30 of Western Airlines and shown at London Gatwick Airport, was a sequel to the international expansion of many United States airlines in the 1970s and 1980s. Western was to be merged into Delta in 1987. In October 1980, it commenced a Honolulu-Anchorage-London service and, in April 1981, a Denver-London service. Both were short-lived.

Eight

WESTERN AIRLINES

Delta's April 1987 acquisition of Western Airlines for $860 million transformed an already huge operation into a truly nationwide airline. It also added a huge history and heritage that had largely centered on the western states and dated back to the 1920s with Pacific Marine Airways and Western Air Express (WAE). Western was known pre-merger as "America's Senior Airline." Founded on July 13, 1925, by Harris Hanshue, WAE benefited from the passing of the Contract Air Mail Act (the Kelly Act). Western successfully bid for CAM.4, commencing its mail service on April 17, 1926, and using three Douglas M-2s, flying from Vail Field in Los Angeles to Salt Lake City via Las Vegas. Western added passenger service on this route on May 23, 1926.

Western commenced flying 12-seat Fokker F-10s between Los Angeles and San Francisco on May 26, 1928. Standard Air Lines was founded in February 1926 and, in November the following year, commenced a scheduled passenger service between Los Angeles and Tucson via Phoenix and a route extended to El Paso via Douglas in February 1929. West Coast Air Transport was another new airline that linked San Francisco with Portland beginning in March 1928. WAE also acquired Mid Continent Air Express and the Colorado Airways, so that by 1930, its network stretched from Kansas City to Los Angeles and from Seattle and Denver to El Paso, a sizeable portion of the southwest United States.

A shotgun marriage between WAE and Transcontinental Air Transport (TAT) in July 1930 resulted in the first TWA, Transcontinental and Western Air. Hanshue lasted only eight months as TWA president. The Mid Continent Air Express element of TWA was of little interest to TWA's coast-to-coast ambitions, and with WAE still nominally trading and with Hanshue still active in the company, WAE was revitalized in October 1931 with the takeover of Mid Continent. General Motor Corporation took controlling interest in WAE and its name changed to General Air Lines in 1934. WAE was divorced from its association with TWA late in 1934, and the Western Air Express Corporation was formed, including a close association with United Air Lines and its fleet of new Boeing 247s.

National Parks Airways was acquired by Western in August 1937 (Salt Lake City to Great Falls, Montana). Then Wyoming Air Service, which became Inland Air Lines in 1938, came under the Western flag in June 1944. During 1941, Western's last links with United were severed.

In a completely different evolution, Alaskan airline, Woodley Airways—founded by Arthur G. Woodley—became Pacific Northern Airways (PNA) in August 1945, changing its name to Pacific Northern Airlines two years later. With Douglas DC-4s acquired in 1947, PNA services from Anchorage to Seattle were launched in October. Lockheed 749A Constellations were added by Woodley in 1955, followed by Boeing 720 services in April 1962. A merger with Western Airlines was agreed by Woodley, completed in July 1967.

Western expanded rapidly in the 1960s, 1970s, and 1980s, even inaugurating a transatlantic service with Douglas DC-10s between Honolulu, Anchorage, and London (Gatwick) in October 1980. A Denver-to-London service was also flown in 1981. Western developed its hub operation in Salt Lake City, incorporating commuter feeder services of SkyWest Airlines. Western was also fielding takeover bids from several airlines, including Continental and Air Florida, and in turn Western had also tried to acquire Wien Air Alaska in 1982. When the Western-Delta merger was completed in April 1987, Delta Air Lines had become the fourth largest airline in the United States and fifth in the world.

A stunning Lucille Ball is shown here in the early 1930s after a flight on a Western Air Express Fokker F-10. Western Air Express's primary route, known as "The Model Airway," was between Los Angeles and San Francisco (Oakland).

This Boeing 204 of Western Air Express was introduced on the airline's Alhambra (Los Angeles)–Long Beach–Avalon (Catalina Island) service in 1929. Before this, from 1922 to June 1928, Pacific Marine Airways had served Avalon with several different seaplane types, including the Curtiss HS-2L. Even before Pacific Marine—which Western took over—Syd Chaplin, elder brother of Charlie Chaplin, had operated the Chaplin Air Line in 1919 and 1920, renamed Catalina Airlines until the Pacific Marine takeover.

The unique and unusual Keystone-Loening C-2H Air Yacht NC9773 is pictured off Catalina Island while flying for Western Air Express shortly after their takeover of Pacific Marine Airways in June 1928. Western also flew three Curtiss HS-2Ls in the late 1920s.

Western Airlines was called "America's Oldest Airline" within the industry until its merger with Delta. Its roots go back to Western Air Express, founded on July 13, 1925, and even earlier if you consider the genealogy back to Chaplin Air Line (see bottom photo and caption on page 70). This Western Air Express Fokker F-14 NC150H is an unusual parasol-wing monoplane, painted in the airline's colors in 1930; however, it was never flown with the airline.

With Western Air Express's unique hexagonal hangar in Los Angeles (Alhambra) in the background, their Boeing 40B-4 NC843M was one of two operated. This one was delivered in March 1930 but crashed in February 1932.

Western Air Express ordered six Douglas M-2 biplanes to operate the CAM-4 mail route from Vail Field, Los Angeles, to Salt Lake City. The first mail service was inaugurated on April 17, 1926, and the first passenger was carried on May 23. This M-2 restoration is seen outside Western's hangar in the early 1950s; a Convair 240 is visible behind.

The same Douglas M-2 biplane restoration as in the picture above is shown here airborne over rural countryside on its way to the Smithsonian Institution. The pilot for the first April 1926 flight was Maury Graham with 256 pounds of mail carried in the forward cockpit area. Simultaneously, a second Douglas M-2 with Jimmie James as pilot departed Salt Lake City for the 653-mile flight to Los Angeles. Eight hours later, both M-2s had landed safely and one commentator remarked, "people might some day pay to travel by air."

Boeing 95 "Mailplane" NC421E was one of four that were delivered to Western Air Express in March and April 1929. This coincided with route expansion with a new service to Albuquerque via Kingman and Holbrook on May 15 and the extension of this service to Kansas City via Amarillo and Wichita on June 1.

Stearman 4DM NC774H (c/n 4011) is pictured at the Stearman factory in Wichita, Kansas, prior to delivery to Western Air Express in March 1930. It was delivered to Western as a three-seater (note the large, one-piece front windshield). The front cockpit was often interchanged with a mail compartment, making it similar to a 4CM.

Sixty-eight years later, this Stearman 4DM was still flying in the colors of Western Air Express, lovingly restored by Jim Kimball and displayed here by owners Carol and Ron Rex, among other antique airplanes in April 1998 at the Sun 'n Fun Fly-In in Lakeland, Florida. This aircraft is fitted with a 400-horsepower Pratt & Whitney Wasp C engine. Although marked as NC774H, the aircraft was in fact NC796H, which in 1937 flew with Wyoming Air Service (later named Inland Air), before being merged with Western Airlines.

For a brief period in 1934, Western Air Express operated the unusual, 10-passenger Clark General Aviation GA-43 as part of their "Rocky Mountain Division," and they are seen here at Denver Municipal Airport. The other unit was the "Pacific Coast Division."

Newly independent Western Air Express, Inc. operated a large fleet of Boeing 247Ds with 34 examples serving the airline between December 1934 and 1941, following the airline's withdrawal from an association with TWA. NC13315 was delivered in June 1935 when this picture was taken.

Waco EQC-6 was a 1936 model, the most powerful of the company's custom cabin models built that year. Wacos were generally sold to corporate or private owners, although a few served as early air taxis with airlines. This aircraft, NC17469, is pictured in 1937.

The Mainliner, a Douglas DST (Douglas Sleeper Transport), operated the Boulder Dam route in joint Western-United colors, following the 1940 launch of an interchange program between the two airlines.

A former Inland Air Lines Lockheed L-18 Lodestar is shown in the colors of Western Airlines, following the merger of Inland with Western in 1944. Inland had been given an ex-Western Lodestar when its Boeing 247s were taken over by the military. This aircraft was used primarily on the Cheyenne–Great Falls route, linking Wyoming and Montana.

NC25634, an Inland Air Lines Lockheed L-18 Lodestar that one of two Inland planes acquired in June 1942, was interchanged with Western (see above). The picture was taken in front of Inland Air Lines hangar in Cheyenne, Wyoming.

Western used two North American AT-6s (Texan) specifically to carry airmail in 1946 and 1947; a third AT-6 was used for spares. They were used by its "Inland Division," part of the route network of Inland Air Lines linking Denver with cities in Wyoming and South Dakota.

Alfred Frank and associates founded National Parks Airways in March 1928 and began operations on August 1, 1928, flying airmail on the CAM.26 route between Salt Lake City and Great Falls, Montana. Initially, three Fokker Super-Universals, of which NC6769 is pictured, and two Stearman C3Bs were flown on the 500-mile route, carrying both mail and passengers.

Two Boeing 40B-4s were operated by National Parks Airways, acquired in 1930 and 1931. During 1930, 16 intermediate landing fields were established along the Salt Lake City–to–Great Falls route throughout the year, and this aircraft, NC841M, was equipped with skis for winter operations.

Standard Airlines commenced scheduled services linking Los Angeles with Tucson, via Phoenix, on November 28, 1927; a route extended to Douglas and El Paso on February 4, 1929. In El Paso, connections were made with the Texas & Pacific Railroad, and eventually with the New York Central Railroad, offering an air-rail transcontinental travel time of 43 hours and 40 minutes. Fokker F-7 NC7888, known as *The Texan*, was used. Standard was acquired by Western Air Express in May 1930.

Aero Corporation of California (ACC) operated Standard Airlines as a subsidiary. Fokker Super-Universals were flown by ACC, carrying six passengers. ACC was also a Fokker distributor on the west coast. Western acquired both ACC and Standard in April 1930. The photo shows a reversible propeller being demonstrated at the Western Aircraft Show in Los Angeles, held November 9–17, 1929.

Mid-Continent Air Express started operations linking Denver with El Paso on September 21, 1929, using a Fokker F-14. Fokker Super-Universals were added later, including NC9724 pictured. Mid-Continent was absorbed by Western Air Express in October 1931.

Fokker F-10A of West Coast Air Transport is pictured in Seattle in 1929. West Coast commenced passenger services between San Francisco (Alameda) and Portland, Oregon, on March 5, 1928, a route soon extended north to Seattle. Western Air Express acquired West Coast in 1929 but in December 1930 had to sell it to Pacific Air Transport (a predecessor of United Air Lines).

Wyoming Air Service linked with Border Airlines of Great Falls, Montana, in 1931 to operate various Stinson monoplane models as Wyoming-Montana Air Lines. When Border stopped flying, the airline became Wyoming Air Service, and still with Stinsons, started flying an airmail route between Pueblo, Colorado, and Cheyenne, Wyoming. Following route expansion and acquisition of Boeing 247s, Wyoming changed its name to Inland Air Lines on July 1, 1938. This line-up of Wyoming Air Service Stinson SM-8As is in 1931.

Only two Boeing Model 200 Monomails were built. They were later converted to eight-passenger aircraft and re-designated the Boeing 221A. They flew with United Air Lines in the 1930s, but on May 24, 1935, were acquired by Wyoming Air Service-Inland Air Lines.

Wyoming Air Service leased a Boeing 247 from United in 1935. In 1938, Wyoming Air Service acquired a further three Boeing 247s, just before being renamed Inland Air Lines. Here "Miss Black Hills," Dorothy Soldab, poses in front of an Inland Boeing 247 in Sturgis, South Dakota, c. 1939.

Another part of the Western jigsaw was founded in Alaska in April 1932 as a small unscheduled charter airline by Arthur C. Woodley. Woodley Airways was founded for mail operations within Alaska, and subsequently for passengers. In July and August 1944, Woodley acquired two Boeing 247Ds from the USAAF, this one pictured in spring 1945. In August 1945, Woodley changed its name to Pacific Northern Airways

As well as its Boeing 247Ds, Woodley operated many other aircraft: Stinson As, Travel Air S-6000s, a Consolidated Fleetster, and this Lockheed 10A.

Pacific Northern's Boeing 247s were replaced in 1946 by a fleet of Douglas DC-3Ds and converted military C-47s. As Alaska's first CAB-certificated airline, Pacific Northern was able to expand its route structure from its Anchorage base southeast to Juneau. NC37469 was delivered in February 1946.

Granting of traffic rights between Anchorage and Seattle required a suitable aircraft. The first of four Douglas DC-4s arrived in July 1951 to inaugurate the Seattle service on October 1. Pacific Northern was now known as the Alaska Flag Line.

Pacific Northern's—and hence Western's—link with Delta started in March 1955 when the Alaskan airline leased (then purchased) three former Delta Lockheed 749A Constellations. The first was N86524, seen here over downtown Seattle.

Over Seattle's futuristic 1962 Space Needle, Arthur Woodley also had a futuristic outlook for his Pacific Northern Airlines. On April 27, 1962, he started Boeing 720 jet service from Seattle to Juneau and Ketchikan. In 1966, a merger with Western Airlines was agreed and completed by July 1, 1967. The three Boeing 720s he had acquired passed to Western but were then sold to Alaska Airlines.

Two of the former Pacific Northern Airlines Lockheed 749A Constellations that were transferred to Western after the 1967 merger were withdrawn from service by December of the following year. The Western Red Indian-head logo of the 1950s can be seen on the forward fuselage of N86525.

Western acquired its first Douglas DC-4s in 1946 to complement the ten Convair 240s it acquired in 1948. It was Terrell C. Drinkwater who headed up Western from 1947 until 1970 and was responsible for its successful growth. Western acquired a large 31-aircraft Douglas DC-6B fleet between 1952 and 1958. N93117 is seen here following its October 1956 delivery to Western; it was sold to Japan Air Lines in February 1962.

Western was late off the mark with orders for the turbo-prop Lockheed 188A Electra. American and Eastern had been operating the new four-engine type for nearly a year before Western's first aircraft, N7135C (pictured), was delivered in May 1959. By 1959, Western had inaugurated its long-awaited service to Calgary, Canada, retired all but one of its DC-3s, signed contracts for Boeing 720s and 707s, and recorded $5 million profit. The dark side was Electra design problems, with engine-related wing vibrations causing the September 29 loss of a Braniff Electra over Buffalo, Texas. The problem was solved by December 1960, but Western subsequently designated its aircraft, Electra IIs.

At Boeing's Renton, Seattle plant, prior to its April 1961 delivery, Boeing 720-047B N9314B became N93141. Western operated a 27-aircraft fleet of the 140-seat Boeing 720s. The 720 was ordered primarily for Western's established routes between Los Angeles and Minneapolis and Los Angeles and Mexico City, as well as its anticipated route between Los Angeles to Hawaii. The last Western 720 service was on January 6, 1980, between Seattle and Los Angeles.

Western leased two Boeing 707-139s that had been earmarked for Cubana Airlines, between May 1960 and September 1962. Five Boeing 707-347Cs were also ordered but were not delivered until June and September 1968; N1502W was the second of these.

Western's first Boeing 737-200, N4501W is shown here at Los Angeles International in June 1968, the month that it first entered service. A company Boeing 720 is behind, along with the famous circular Theme Building.

Competition in the Pacific seaboard markets was intense, notably from Pacific Southwest Airlines and United. The Boeing 737 was the right aircraft for the job, and Western's fleet of 737s grew to number 58 different aircraft, including several ex-Delta 737s. This is an air-to-air picture of Western's first 737-200, N4501W.

The fourth Boeing jet to join the Western fleet was the 727-247. N2801W was the first, delivered on October 16, 1969, and the last, N296WA, was brought in June 1981 after 46 had been delivered. A former Western 727-200, N283WA flew Delta's last revenue scheduled service between Greensboro, North Carolina and Atlanta on April 6, 2003.

As machinations over Western's ownership occurred in the late 1960s and early 1970s, a merger with American Airlines was quashed by the CAB in 1972. The year 1970 was also time for an image change at Delta when its new "W" *Swizzle Stick* colors were first introduced. The newly delivered Boeing 737-200, N4530W shows this new color scheme to perfection.

Most of Western's fleet were painted with the "W" *swizzle-stick* color scheme. The fifth of Western's Boeing 707-347Cs, N1505W (above) was delivered in September 1968.

A May 1972 delivery, this Boeing 727-247 was transferred to Delta in the 1987 merger. However, it was retired by Delta in 1999 and moved to desert storage in Victorville, California.

This pair of Boeing 727-247s, N2829W and N2810W, are pictured in April 1982 at Los Angeles International Airport (LAX). Western grew its LAX operation in the early 1980s, particularly with links to its other hub in Salt Lake City.

On final approach to land at Las Vegas McCarran Field in April 1982 is Western Boeing 727-247 N2825W. Western's strength in the western United States concerned many of its rival airlines; highly prized was Western's Salt Lake City hub, the original point served by Western Air Express in 1926, but also its strategic location in the United States, away from United and Continental's dominance in Denver.

Western's first Douglas DC-10-10 was delivered in April 1973. Western was the only airline competing in the California-to-Hawaii market in the early 1970s and not flying a wide-body jet. Therefore, Fred Benninger, Western senior executive, chose the DC-10 over the Boeing 747 for this route while discussions continued over a possible merger with American. The DC-10-30 N821L was leased from Air New Zealand in the early 1980s for Western's new service from Denver Stapleton to London Gatwick.

A third change of image for Western was introduced in 1984 with a bare metal scheme, restyled "W" and restyled titling for "Western," as shown on this Boeing 737-247 Advanced N236WA. Delta's $860-million acquisition of Western was completed operationally on April 1, 1987, transforming Delta in to the United States' fourth largest and the world's fifth largest airline.

Nine

1990s, the Shuttle, Connection, and Express

Delta's jigsaw of mergers and acquisitions appeared complete, but the failure of PanAm afforded gains for others. In 1991, several of PanAm's assets were acquired by Delta, including their transatlantic routes and related "beyond" rights, strategic landing-takeoff slots, and its fleet of Airbus A310s. PanAm's Frankfurt hub was also acquired, along with the "Shuttle," the high frequency services flown between Washington, New York, and Boston, and competing on the same northeast corridor routes with the Trump Shuttle, soon to be taken over by USAir (now US Airways).

Commuter or feeder services to the big airline hub airports developed in the United States from the 1960s onwards. Delta through growth and mergers has developed five main hubs: Atlanta Hartsfield International, Cincinnati-Northern Kentucky International, Salt Lake City, Dallas-Ft. Worth, and New York City (JFK). Providing feed to these hubs from a range of market sizes required a range of aircraft, and while Delta's mainline fleet of Boeings and MD aircraft could adequately handle the feed from bigger markets, the smaller towns and cities required a different formula. Franchising the Delta name to smaller independent commuter airlines was the solution. It was in March 1984 that Atlantic Southeast Airlines (ASA) first entered a code-share agreement with Delta, feeding mainly the Atlanta hub. Soon after, in Cincinnati in September 1984, Comair did the same. At JFK, Ransome Airlines and Trans States Airlines did the same. In Salt Lake City, it was SkyWest Airlines, and in Dallas-Ft. Worth, it was Rio Airways, which were soon assimilated into ASA. Other Delta Connection carriers are Business Express, which joined on June 1, 1986; Atlantic Coast Airlines (ACA), which joined on August 1, 2000; American Eagle, which joined on January 18, 2002; and Chautauqua Airlines, which joined on November 1, 2002.

Delta Connection airlines grew rapidly; by 1998, ASA had a fleet of 80 aircraft and 2,500 employees and were receiving their first jets, Canadair RJ-100s. Comair was even larger with 92 aircraft and 3,200 employees, and it already had 53 Canadair RJ-100 jets. In 1999, Delta acquired 100-percent ownership of both ASA and Comair, and in March 2000, Delta and Bombardier (manufacturer of the Canadair RJ) announced the largest regional jet order in history with 94 firm orders for RJ-200s and RJ-700s. By July 2003, ASA had a fleet of 100 Canadair RJs and, by December 2004, expect that the three main connection carriers will have a combined Canadair RJ fleet totaling 343 aircraft.

Low-fare airlines emerged as vibrant and respected forces in the United States domestic market in the 1990s. SouthWest Airlines was growing steadily and profitably, and Delta sought to provide its own low-fare unit, establishing Delta Express in October 1996, initially targeting the Florida leisure market from Orlando, 4 other Florida cities, and 10 northeastern and Midwest cities. Boeing 737-200s were transferred from the mainline fleet and configured in a 119-seat, one-class layout. Cabin crews wore casual clothes, turn-arounds were quick, and aircraft utilization high. Delta Express operated until 2003, when Delta replaced it with a new low-fare unit named Song.

Delta was the official airline of the 1996 Olympic Games in Atlanta. Leo F. Mullin was appointed Delta's president and CEO in August 1997, and soon after, on December 22, Margaret Mack entered aviation history when she boarded a Delta flight from Dallas-Ft. Worth to Atlanta and became Delta's 100-millionth customer that year, a feat never before achieved by an airline in a year. That year, Delta enplaned 103,295,376 passengers. It was also the year that Delta changed its livery after 35 years of the traditional widget and signed a 10-year exclusivity deal with Boeing (soon extended to 20 years) for the supply of up to 644 new Boeing aircraft. Orders were placed in 1997 for ten Boeing 777-200s as well.

When McDonnell Douglas stretched, modernized, and re-engined its DC-10 in the 1980s, the MD-11 was born. Delta, seeking a suitable long-range, 276-seat aircraft to replace Tristars on transpacific routes and to develop new transpacific and transatlantic routes, initially ordered nine MD-11s with options on a further 31. In the end, only 15 MD-11s were delivered to Delta, two of which are pictured at London Gatwick in March 1998.

Delta's first McDonnell Douglas MD-11 touches down at Atlanta Hartsfield International Airport in November 1990. This is one of two, leased MD-11s flown by Delta pending delivery of their first aircraft late in 1991. The MD-11s' career with Delta has been relatively short, due to fleet rationalization, the last being retired from the fleet early in 2004.

As a result of Delta's acquisition of some of PanAmerican's assets in 1991, it operated some ex-PanAm Airbus A310-200s and A310-300s, including N805PA, seen here in Atlanta in 1992. This aircraft was sold to small-package carrier Federal Express in 1994. The remainder of the Airbus fleet were also disposed of.

In 1996, Atlanta hosted the Olympic Games. Not surprisingly, Delta became the official airline of the games and, in celebration, painted two of its aircraft in special colors. MD-11 N812DE (marked here, pre-delivery, as N6202S) was one of these.

The second of Delta's two aircraft painted in special 1996 *Olympic Games* colors was Boeing 767-232 N102DA, *Spirit of Delta*, the first of the airline's 767s purchased with funds raised by Delta employees in 1983 (see Chapter 7).

A major new type to join Delta's fleet during the 1990s was the large, twin-engine Boeing 777-200, also known as a "Triple Seven." The first "Triple Seven," part of an order for twelve, was delivered from Seattle to Atlanta on March 29, 1999, although initially only two were operated, some on transatlantic routes, because of flight-deck crewing difficulties.

With the retirement of Delta president Ronald W. Allen, who had been with Delta for 34 years, 54-year-old Leo F. Mullin was appointed Delta's president and CEO in August 1997. Fred Reid took over his position as president (and COO), and at the end of 2003, Mullin is Delta's chairman and chief executive officer.

Another legacy of PanAm's demise in 1991 was Delta's takeover of the "PanAm Shuttle" and acquisition of PanAm's remaining Atlantic route network in a $416-million deal. With 14, dedicated Boeing 727s, the Delta Shuttle commenced on September 1, 1991, on the Boston–New York–Washington corridor, flying 64 scheduled flights each weekday.

With the retirement of Boeing 727s, the Delta Shuttle was also equipped with new aircraft from 1998 onwards, namely new generation Boeing 737s. Pictured is N3732J, one of 16 Boeing 737-832s now dedicated to shuttle.

In 1997, the Delta Shuttle boarded over 2 million passengers and, in April that year, achieved the boarding milestone of its 10 millionth shuttle customer. Use of the Boeing 737-832, including N3738B, pictured here, has reduced noise and increased operational efficiency. Shuttle passengers are primarily on business, take at least four shuttle flights a year, and nearly one half of them live in the New York-New Jersey area.

Simultaneously with Leo Mullins's appointment as CEO in 1997, Delta took the bold decision to abandon its widget color scheme that had served it for 35 years and adopted a new Landor-designed scheme. Boeing 767-332 N190DN was the first aircraft to wear the scheme; here it is worn by Delta's Boeing 737-35B N224DA (an ex-Germanair 737, D-AGED), seen in Cincinnati in May 2000.

Another major 1990s Delta innovation was its Business Elite class, with leather seating and the best seat pitch in the industry. First introduced on Boeing 767s and the new 777s in 1999, Business Elite was a move away from the more traditional three-class seating on long haul flights to a two-class system.

Following the lead of Ransome Airlines (see Chapter 7), Delta also entered a code-share agreement with Atlantic Southeast Airlines (ASA) in March 1984. The code share meant that ASA could use the "DL" Delta reservations code on flights that connected with Delta mainline flights. ASA initially flew between Atlanta and Columbus, Macon, and Athens, and used DHC-6 Twin Otters and Embraer EMB-110 Bandeirantes. By the time this 1991 photo was taken, ASA was flying a large network of feeder flights, the Delta Connection, into Delta's hubs in Atlanta and Dallas-Ft. Worth with Embraer EMB-120 Brasilias and a few DHC-7s.

Soon after ASA signed a code share, Cincinnati-based Comair also signed one with Delta on September 1, 1984, to become a Delta Connection carrier centered on Cincinnati and Orlando. This is a Comair Embraer EMB-110 Bandeirante that served the Orlando hub.

In the western United States, Delta inherited a new Delta Connection carrier, Skywest Airlines, when it merged with Western in 1987. Skywest operated Swearingen SA.227 Metroliners and built its operations at Delta's Salt Lake City hub and at LAX. N27240 Metroliner is seen here at John Wayne-Orange County Airport in June 1994.

Following Delta's code-share agreement with Skywest, it expanded its fleet with Embraer EMB-120 Brasilia turbo-props. By the late 1990s, Skywest was offering more daily departures from LAX than any other airline, serving eight western states with over 294 daily flights to 48 cities.

Other commuter operators were keen to sign code-share agreements with airlines such as Delta. In the northeastern United States, Business Express, operating a fleet of Saab 340A twin turbo-props, became a Delta Connection carrier in July 1986, serving Delta at New York-LaGuardia and Boston.

Pictured at Washington National in November 1998 in a later and revised livery, passengers deplane from a Business Express (BEX) Saab 340A. The vagaries of commuter airlines and code-share agreements saw BEX change allegiance, and in 1999, American Eagle acquired the airline.

Established in Cincinnati in 1977 by David Mueller, Comair had virtually replaced its Piper PA-31s by 1985 with a mixed fleet of EMB-110 Bandeirantes, Saab-Fairchild SF.340s, Shorts SD-3-30s, and Swearingen SA.227 Metro IIIs. Two of the latter are pictured in 1995 at the airline's Orlando hub.

Also at Comair's Orlando hub are two Embraer EMB-120 Brasilias. Comair ordered the 30-seat Brasilias in 1990, the same year that it inaugurated its second hub in Orlando, Florida.

With two 1,800-horsepower Pratt & Whitney PW118 turboprops, the Brazilian-built, pressurized Embraer EMB-120 Brasilia proved an ideal type for the burgeoning United States commuter airline industry in the 1980s. Its maximum cruise speed is 313 miles per hour (504 kilometers per hour). Delta Connection Comair operated a fleet of 30 Brasilias, all of which had been retired by 2001.

Comair operated a dense network of feeder routes as Delta Connection from its Cincinnati-Northern Kentucky base. Destinations served stretched from Toronto in the north to Birmingham, Alabama, in the south. This Comair Saab SF.340A was one of 19 they operated in the late 1980s and early 1990s, and is pictured in Toronto.

The Embraer EMB-120 Brasilia commuter liner first flew on July 27, 1983. Atlantic Southeast Airlines (ASA) was launch customer for the type, their first aircraft entering service in October 1985. In Delta's most recent colors, this ASA Brasilia is pictured in Atlanta. The ASA-Delta Connection retired their last Brasilia on July 31, 2003, its final service being DL4123 from Wichita to Delta's Dallas-Ft. Worth hub.

ASA's other turboprop is the French-Italian-built, 68-seat ATR-72. In the early 1990s, ASA had planned to operate a fleet of up to 20 British-built BAe.146 regional jets, but after operating a small number of them for two years, ASA changed tack and standardized on the ATR-72, with 20 acquired, and Canadair RJ-100s. This ATR-72 is pictured landing in Atlanta in March 1999.

Comair's first regional jets were delivered in 1994, Bombardier Canadair RJ100ERs, one of which is seen here in June 1995 landing at the Twin Cities, Minneapolis-St. Paul. Delta acquired a 20 percent shareholding in Comair, operating as the Delta Connection, in July 1986.

Comair became an all-jet Delta Connection airline at its Cincinnati-Northern Kentucky hub in 2000. To mark the occasion, it painted its Bombardier CRJ-100 (also designated a Canadair CL-600-2B19) N729CA, fleet No.7265, in special *Cincinnati—The Jet Hub* colors.

Regional jets have revolutionized the United States commuter airline industry, opening up markets that would never have been considered viable with turboprops. Delta Connection carrier Comair is now a wholly jet operator. Delta acquired 100 percent ownership of Comair on November 22, 1999.

With Comair and ASA, which also became 100 percent owned by Delta in 1999, operating similar Bombardier-Canadair regional jet types, aircraft interchange is possible to make up for short-falls. Although Comair does not normally operate in Delta's Atlanta hub, this Comair CRJ-100 is seen in Atlanta in June 2003 operating an ASA flight.

Delta Connection carrier ASA started to reequip with regional jets later than Comair. The first of the Bombardier/Canadair CRJ.100s were delivered in early 2000, and two examples are pictured here in Atlanta fresh from the factory. The rapid growth in regional jet traffic in Atlanta is the main reason that precipitated the decision to construct a fifth parallel runway at the world's busiest airport.

By March 2003, Delta Connection carrier ASA had a large and growing fleet of regional jets at its Atlanta and Dallas-Ft. Worth hubs. On March 29, 2000, Delta and Bombardier announced the largest regional jet order in history, with 94 CRJ200 and CRJ700 aircraft, plus 406 options. The 100th Bombardier regional jet was delivered to ASA on July 2, 2003. ASA's Bombardier-Canadair CRJ.100s serve 82 destinations from Atlanta and 37 from Dallas-Ft. Worth.

Delta's domination of activity at its Atlanta hub is evident here in this June 2003 picture. In 2002, ASA started to take delivery of the stretched version of the CRJ100, the CRJ700, a 70-seater. The prototype first flew on May 27, 1999, and two of the jets are pictured here in the foreground. By the end of 2004, Delta Connection carriers ASA, Comair, and SkyWest will be operating 343 CRJs.

To counteract competition from the upsurge in new low-fare airlines in the United States, including Southwest Airline, Delta set up its own low-fare unit, Delta Express. Operations commenced, using Boeing 737-200s, on October 1, 1996, only five months after the new concept had first been discussed.

Delta Express was initially planned and headed by W.E. "Skip" Barnette (now ASA president) and Paulette Corbin. They were the focus for a major front-line initiative at Delta for all staff to look at the airline's products with a view to improvement. Florida leisure markets were those identified quickly as ripe for low-fare action by Delta. This Delta Express Boeing 737-200 is seen landing in Tampa, one of five Florida destinations served.

N305DL Boeing 737-247 of Delta Express is shown at the gate in Orlando in 1998. Immediately at its launching, Delta Express was operating 62 daily flights with a high aircraft utilization, exceeding 12 hours in-flight per aircraft per day.

Casual uniforms were the order of the day for Delta Express cabin crews, a culture that took some adjusting among traditionalists. The signature low-fare ethos that Delta Express embraced included one-class seating, 30-minute turn-arounds, no complementary in-flight catering, and of course, some of the lowest fare levels in the market.

Delta Express survived until early 2003, when a major reconsideration of the concept, combined with the rapid growth and success of competitors such as New York–based JetBlue, caused its closure. The new concept was a low-cost carrier called Song.

Ten

SKYTEAM ALLIANCE
AND THE 21ST CENTURY

Global synergies of the world's airlines caused them to form alliances. These alliances became dominant in the last decade of the 20th century, stimulated by the big United States–based airlines jockeying for position and trying to increase market share over their rivals. Delta Air Lines was one of these, forming the Skyteam alliance in 2000, initial membership comprising Delta, Air France, Aeromexico, and Korean Air. CSA Czech Airlines and Alitalia joined more recently.

Airline alliances are in no way a new idea. In the formative years of U.S. air transport, airlines formed alliances with the railroad companies. In 1928, to achieve a transcontinental link (east to west coast), TWA predecessor TAT teamed with the Santa Fe Railroads and Pennsylvania Railroad. Passengers from New York to Los Angeles rode the train west to Columbus, Ohio, flew on to Waynoka, Texas, then took the train again to Clovis, New Mexico, and completed their journey from there to Los Angeles by air. Delta experienced several alliances already, the interchange arrangement with PanAm in the 1960s and 1970s being a prime example (see Chapter 7).

September 11, 2001, will forever be a watershed in air transport history. Delta has been affected as dramatically as most other airlines worldwide. Fleet rationalization and the furloughing of large numbers of pilots and other loyal staff was unfortunately a commercial necessity.

By July 2003, Delta Air Lines was the world's second largest airline in terms of passengers carried and the leading United States carrier across the Atlantic. Despite the effects of 9/11, Delta still offers its customers an unrivalled 5,734 flights each day to 444 destinations in 79 countries, carried on mainline Delta, Song, Delta Shuttle, Delta Connection, and Delta's worldwide partners.

More information on Delta can be obtained from their web site : www.delta.com. Information on other Delta memorabilia and enthusisast products can be found at www. dalstore.com.

Formed on June 22, 2000, initially at the instigation of Delta and partner Air France, the quartet of Skyteam alliance founder airlines were Delta, Air France, Aeromexico, and Korean Air. The six-airline alliance now operates over 7,979 daily flights to over 512 destinations worldwide in 114 countries.

Air France serves more international destinations from its Paris-Charles de Gaulle airport than any of the other five Skyteam members. This Boeing 777-228ER, one of 24 "triple sevens" in the Air France fleet, is seen on arrival in Atlanta from Charles de Gaulle. In mid-2003, reports persisted that Air France would forge an alliance with Dutch airline KLM and bring it within the Skyteam umbrella.

Aeromexico Boeing 757-2Q8 N804AM touches down at Atlanta Hartsfield International Airport on arrival from Mexico City. When Aeromexico scaled down its operations to Europe in the mid-1990s, the airline formed its first relationship with Air France. The airline's origins go back to 1934 and Aeronavas de Mexico; the current name was only adopted in 1972. The original Aeromexico was declared bankrupt in the late 1980s, and a new airline was formed under its former name.

Korean Air's safety record of the last decade has now been addressed, and 80 percent of the airline's traffic is now originating from domestic and Japanese routes. This Boeing 747-400 is seen landing at London Heathrow Airport. Korean Air also signed a Memorandum of Understanding at the 2003 Paris Air Show for five of the huge, 500-seat Airbus A380s, with options on another three for delivery from 2007 through to 2009.

Italian international airline Alitalia, whose roots go back to 1946, became the sixth Skyteam member in July 2001. Alitalia's main base is in Rome and its main hub is located at Milan Malpensa. This MD-82, I-DANW *Siena*, is pictured in Barcelona in February 2003.

CSA Czech Airlines was founded in 1923. With the division of Czechoslovakia in 1995, the airline started to replace its predominantly Soviet fleet with western aircraft. Two Airbus A310-300s were flown on transatlantic routes but will soon be replaced. CSA Czech joined Skyteam in March 2001.

Despite the dramatic effects of September 11 on most of the major airlines in the United States, including considerable financial loses, Delta Air Lines has coped with these traumatic events better than many of its compatriots. Delta's international reach in the early 21st century has remained an important element of its philosophy, despite the opportunities of Skyteam. This Boeing 767-300 is in Zurich, Switzerland, one of 32 markets around the world that Delta serves.

Delta introduced another new color scheme in March 2000, only three years after the 1997 image change; it is seen here on a Boeing 757-232 in Atlanta in 2002. The widget logo was modified and the words "Air Lines" omitted from the fuselage, leaving just the single word "Delta." Fred Reid said of the new colors, "Ultimately we are evolving as an airline, and our look has to evolve with it . . . the new look builds on an illustrious heritage and positions us for the future."

This image displays the post-2000 colors of Delta on the tail of a Boeing 757-232 at the gate at SeaTac airport (Seattle-Tacoma International Airport) in Washington State in July 2002, with the snow-capped peak of Mt. Rainier beyond.

Another new color scheme worn by Delta's fleet appeared in 2000 with the airline's official support for another Olympic Games, this time the 2002 Winter Olympics, hosted in another one of Delta's hubs, Salt Lake City. *Soaring Spirit*, Boeing 777-232ER N864DA, fleet number 7005, delivered to Atlanta from Boeing on March 12, 2000, was one of two aircraft to wear a special *2002 Olympic Winter Games* scheme.

Soaring Spirit, Delta's specially painted 2002 Olympic Winter Games Boeing 777-232ER is shown during turn-around at the airline's Cincinnati-Northern Kentucky International Airport hub. The scheme depicted ice speed skaters on the rear fuselage and tail. In summer 2000, Delta was using 777s on their transatlantic schedules from Cincinnati to London.

The second aircraft that Delta painted to promote itself as the official airline sponsor of the 2002 Olympic Winter Games in Salt Lake City was the newly delivered Boeing 757-232 N6701. Also named *Soaring Spirit*, it displayed a different rear fuselage design than the 777.

Delta Boeing 777-232ER N866DA, one of eight in the airline's fleet during 2003, is pictured landing in Atlanta with the downtown tower blocks beyond. Delta anticipated greater use of its triple-seven fleet on international services, but the effects on traffic post-9/11, with diminished loads, has meant most being used on high capacity domestic services.

During 2000 and 2001, Delta used its Boeing 777s—often informally called "the king of airliners"—on many of its long-haul routes but substituted MD-11s as passenger numbers declined. However, with the retirement of MD-11s, the "triple sevens" are again being used more frequently on transatlantic services (along with Boeing 767-300ERs). N862DA, a triple seven, is seen here at London Gatwick in June 2003.

While being slowly phased from service, Delta's fleet of 120 MD-88s will continue in service well beyond the airline's 75th anniversary of passenger services. Their 140-passenger interiors slot them in nicely between smaller Delta Connection regional jets and larger 177 passenger Boeing 737-800s. This MD-88 is taxiing to the gate at Melbourne International Airport on Florida's east coast.

Delta was still loyal to its old friend Douglas (now McDonnell Douglas and before they were bought by Boeing) and sought to increase its short-medium haul capacity. In November 1989, they were launch customer for the new 150-seat McDonnell Douglas MD-90-30, a stretched version of the MD-88 (see preceding photo). As many as 50 were ordered, with options on a further 110. The prototype first flew on February 22, 1993, and Delta took delivery of its first MD-90 two years later. In the end, only 16 MD-90s were delivered to Delta, the options cancelled, and production of the type ceased. This MD-90 is pictured at John Wayne-Orange County in California, a new direct link between this destination and Atlanta having commenced with Boeing 757-232s on October 1, 2003.

Another landmark of 1997 was the deal that Delta signed with Boeing, initially for a ten-year exclusivity deal with the airliner manufacturer as sole supplier to Delta and then as a 20-year agreement. As many as 644 aircraft were signed for, initially as part of Delta's replacement and rationalization of its domestic fleet, covering 106 Boeing aircraft for delivery between 1998 and 2006. Pictured is one of these, Boeing 767-432ER N845MH, which was delivered by Boeing in 2002.

Despite the fleet replacement and rationalization at Delta, older Boeing 737-200s still provided valiant service, and some were painted in the new colors from 2000 onwards. N323DL, originally delivered in June 1984, is seen here at Cincinnati-Northern Kentucky Airport in snowy weather during the winter of 2000. The small cabin suspended above the fuselage of the 737 is part of the airline's de-icing team, which spray de-icing fluid onto the aircraft, essential for safe winter operations and in keeping departures on time.

Another mainstay of Delta's 21st-century fleet is the Boeing 767. The first 767 was delivered to Delta in 1982 and deliveries of the type are still being made, although they are of the super-stretched 767-400. This is 269-seat Boeing 767-332 N143DA touching down in Atlanta.

Ground Ops at Delta's destination airport go on almost unnoticed by the passenger but are an essential prerequisite for punctuality. Here a Boeing 767-332ER N192DN is at push-back from the terminal air bridge on one of the many stands that Delta occupies in Atlanta. The supervisor on the ground has a direct radio link to the captain and two wing-walkers to ensure the route is clear. The radio link is only disconnected from the airliner at the very last moment once the aircraft is able to taxi to the runway under its own power.

The Boeing 737 has taken over from the Boeing 727 and MD-88 as the most numerous aircraft type in the Delta fleet. All models of 737 (Srs. 200, 300, and 800) now number over 130. This Delta 737-832 is seen in company with a MD-88 and Air France Boeing 767-300 in Philadelphia in April 2001.

A Delta Boeing 737-800 taxis to the gate on arrival at Cincinnati-Northern Kentucky in May 2000. Delta first served Cincinnati in 1941 with a service from Savannah, Georgia.

One of Delta's great strengths is its five hub operations in Atlanta, Dallas-Ft. Worth, New York (JFK), Salt Lake City, and Cincinnati (CVG). Pictured at the latter hub are two MD-88s and a Boeing 757-232 in May 2000. In 1981, Delta started development of a hub operation at CVG with 30 flights a day and flew 1,026,464 passengers. By the beginning of the 21st century, Delta's CVG operation accounted for 250 daily flights and transatlantic services to Brussels, Frankfurt, Paris, and London (Gatwick).

Prime among all its five hubs is Delta's Atlanta headquarters and hub, with four parallel runways, soon to be supplemented by a fifth to the south (in the fore-ground). Seen here from 5,000 feet, the Atlanta hub sees about 625 daily Delta jet departures to 125 non-stop destinations.

Atlanta Hartsfield International Airport is the world's busiest, and in 2002, it handled 76.876 million passengers, a 1.3 percent increase from the 2001 figure. As Delta's home base, they represent about 85 percent of these figures. Since 1970, Delta's enplanement traffic in Atlanta has increased every year except 1981, 1982, 1990, and 2001. Of the 105 gates available in Atlanta, Delta uses around 80.

Delta's huge maintenance hangar (the Technical Operations Center, or TOC) at Atlanta Hartsfield International is the world's largest single-span, cantilever building, at 1,600 feet in length, 300 feet wide, and 93 feet high. Here in 1998, it accommodates at least six Delta airliners, including Boeing 767s and 757s, but it can accommodate up to 16 airliners, slotted in nose to tail.

Delta's TOC in Atlanta is always a hive of activity. In July 2003, Delta in conjunction with Skyteam partner Air France, announced their plan to establish maintenance centers of excellence on both sides of the Atlantic to attract more third-party maintenance work. Air France Industries will focus on Airbus and Boeing 747/777 types, while Delta's TOC will specialize in Boeing 737, 757, and 767 aircraft.

Delta's Atlanta hub, known by Delta as "Atlanta Worldport," is described as being "like a huge factory with people, bags, cargo, mail and airplanes being processed through, coming in at one end and despatched out of the other end." Here some of the 100,000 items of baggage dealt with by Delta on a daily basis in Atlanta are handled from aircraft to conveyor belt to baggage trolley, and then to either the connecting flight or the baggage carousel in the terminal.

April 2003 saw the retirement of Delta's last Boeing 727 tri-jet, in its time one of the world's most successful airliners. Here N517DA, a 727-232, touches down in Atlanta at the end of another safe Delta flight.

One of the most recent innovations at Delta has been the creation of a new low-fare unit, Song. The other innovation with Song is the use of Boeing 757-200s in a 199-seat, one-class configuration; most of the United States low-fare airlines use either Boeing 737s or Airbus aircraft. Song was launched on April 15, 2003, with a flight from New York (JFK) to West Palm Beach in Florida.

Delta sees two of its major growth sectors for the future as its smaller Delta Connection services with Bombardier-Canadair CRJ regional jets and its low-fare unit, Song. The Song 757s will appear in four different colors, this one being lime green, but based on the same design. By October 2003, Song planned to be operating 144 flights daily from New York's three airport's—JFK, LaGuardia, and Newark—to Atlanta, Boston, Washington, Fort Myers, Orlando, San Juan, Tampa, West Palm Beach, and Las Vegas.

Final flashback to the days of the widget color scheme: this March 1998 line-up in Atlanta features most of types of aircraft from the Delta fleet of the time. The heady days of the late 1990s were also some of the most profitable at Delta, prior to the dark days of 9/11 when the United States air transport industry reeled from the shock and had to downsize its aircraft fleets, its route structure, and unfortunately its staff. The market continues to be extremely difficult with competition from other carriers proving intense. The positives, as Delta Air Lines celebrates its 75th anniversary of scheduled passenger services, are its resilience and excellence of service. There have been many ups and downs during the years 1929 to 2004—there will doubtless be more—yet Delta Air Lines will continue to survive and fly its millions of customers successfully and safely.

Visit us at
arcadiapublishing.com